Improving Teaching
with Collaborative

action
research

Improving Teaching
with Collaborative
action
research

Diane Cunningham

ASCD® LEARN. TEACH. LEAD.
Alexandria, Virginia USA

1703 North Beauregard St. • Alexandria, VA 22311-1714 USA
Phone: 1-800-933-2723 or 1-703-578-9600 • Fax: 1-703-575-5400
Website: www.ascd.org • E-mail: member@ascd.org
Author guidelines: www.ascd.org/write

Gene R. Carter, *Executive Director;* Judy Zimny, *Chief Program Development Officer;* Gayle Owens, *Managing Director, Content Acquisitions and Development;* Nancy Modrak, *Publisher;* Carolyn Pool, *Content Development;* Gary Bloom, *Managing Director, Creative Services;* Mary Beth Nielsen, *Manager, Editorial Services;* Alicia Goodman, *Project Manager;* Catherine Guyer, *Senior Graphic Designer;* Mike Kalyan, *Manager, Production Services;* Keith Demmons, *Desktop Publishing Specialist;* Kyle Steichen, *Production Specialist*

Printed in the United States of America. Cover art © 2011 by ASCD. ASCD publications present a variety of viewpoints. The views expressed or implied in this book should not be interpreted as official positions of ASCD.

All web links in this book are correct as of the publication date below but may have become inactive or otherwise modified since that time. If you notice a deactivated or changed link, please e-mail books@ascd .org with the words "Link Update" in the subject line. In your message, please specify the web link, the book title, and the page number on which the link appears.

PAPERBACK ISBN: 978-1-4166-1162-2   ASCD Product #111006   n01/11

Quantity discounts for the paperback edition only: 10–49 copies, 10%; 50+ copies, 15%; for 1,000 or more copies, call 1-800-933-2723, ext. 5634, or 1-703-575-5634.

Library of Congress Cataloging-in-Publication Data
Cunningham, Diane, 1962-
  Improving teaching with collaborative action research : an ASCD action tool / Diane Cunningham.
    p. cm.
  ISBN 978-1-4166-1162-2 (pbk. : alk. paper) 1. Action research in education. 2. Teachers--In-service training. 3. Group work in education. I. Title.
  LB1028.24.C86 2011
  370.72--dc22
                    2010041214

18 17 16 15 14 13 12 11   1 2 3 4 5 6 7 8 9 10

Improving Teaching with Collaborative action research

Acknowledgments ix

INTRODUCTION

What Is Collegial Inquiry? 3

Organization of This Action Tool 9

SECTION 1: Fostering Common Understanding of the Collegial Inquiry Process

Defining the Characteristics of Collegial Inquiry 16

Assessing the Quality of a Collegial Inquiry Plan 20

Understanding What Makes Professional Learning
    Communities Successful. 30

Considering Research Validity in Collegial Inquiry 36

Personal Learning Journal 1 41

SECTION 2: Finding a Meaningful Starting Point and Developing Rationale

Identifying Inquiry Topics. 46

Selecting a Topic 48

Ensuring a Meaningful Starting Point. 50

Developing a Rationale 54

Assessing the Quality of Your Rationale 60

Creating a Vision for Success. 62

Personal Learning Journal 2 66

SECTION 3: Generating Inquiry Questions

Two Types of Inquiry: Exploratory and Action Oriented 72

Crafting Inquiry Questions. 76

Designing Inquiry Questions from Stems. 80

Assessing the Quality of Inquiry Questions. 84

Personal Learning Journal 3 88

SECTION 4: Planning for and Taking Action

Planning for Action. 94

Exploring Possible Actions 102

Taking Action and Considering Its Effects 104

Personal Learning Journal 4 107

SECTION 5: Meeting and Ensuring That Discourse Produces Learning

Planning an Inquiry Meeting 112

Creating an Agenda 114

Establishing Ground Rules 120

Facilitating Collegial Inquiry. 122

Keeping an Eye on Discourse 128

Assessing the Quality of Text-Based Discussion. 132

Evaluating Your Contribution to Discussion. 134

Personal Learning Journal 5 136

SECTION 6: Collecting and Analyzing Data

Identifying Data Sources for Collegial Inquiry 142

Matching Data Sources with Inquiry Questions 146

Planning Data Collection 148

Assessing the Quality of Data Collection 152

Organizing Data for Analysis 154

Analyzing Data by Identifying Themes 158

Drawing Conclusions from Data 166

Capturing the Group's Learning from Data Analysis. 170

Personal Learning Journal 6 172

SECTION 7: Fostering Individual and Group Reflection

Gauging the Group's Feelings 178

Thinking About the Inquiry Process Together. 180

Reflecting Creatively 182

Ranking Actions for Value. 186

Reflecting in Small Groups 188

Reflecting on Successes 190

Personal Learning Journal 7 193

About the Author 195

Downloads

Electronic versions of the tools are available for download
at **www.ascd.org/downloads**.

Enter this unique key code to unlock the files:
GBF59 0CD77 EA616

If you have difficulty accessing the files, e-mail webhelp@ascd.org
or call 1-800-933-ASCD for assistance.

Acknowledgments

This action tool is dedicated to the many teachers and administrators who have engaged in the inquiry process honestly and without fear to investigate their practice and learn from one another. Their hard work, sincere questioning, and willingness to persevere have been an ongoing inspiration.

I must also acknowledge my colleagues at Learner-Centered Initiatives Ltd., especially Giselle, Joanne, Angela, Julie, and Jenn, whom I've learned from and with for many years. Their feedback and support have been invaluable.

Finally, I thank my children, Kerin and Andrew, for providing me with purpose every day.

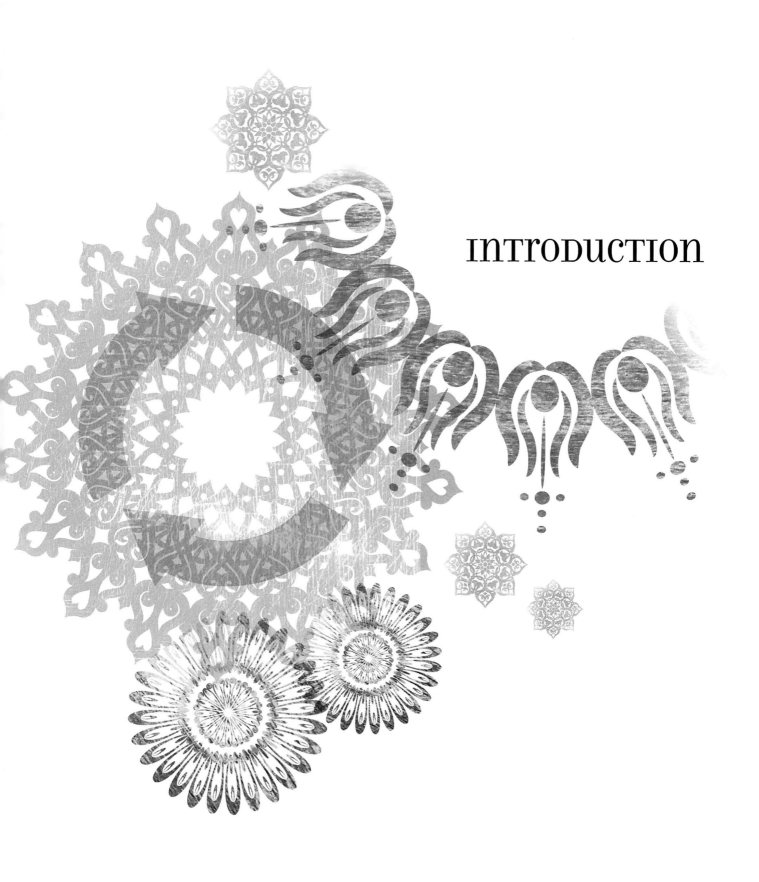

INTRODUCTION

What Is Collegial Inquiry?

Collaborative action research, also known as *collegial inquiry*, can be defined as a learner-centered approach to staff development. It grows from the tradition of action research, which emphasizes the idea that individual and teams of educators can and should study their practice as a means to improve it (Mills, 2007). Action research has a long history in the social sciences and was brought formally to education in 1943 by the Horace Mann-Lincoln Institute for School Experimentation as a process that could close the gap between research knowledge and instructional practices (Richardson, 2001). As a practical professional development approach, collegial inquiry, which is the term I'll be using throughout this book, requires educators in a professional learning community to make decisions about what to study and how to study and to commit to reflective practice.

The collegial inquiry process is different from other forms of collaborative work that educators engage in: Instead of being guided by products, educators using collegial inquiry are guided by questions. Often educators come together to design lessons or curriculum, create programs, or solve school problems. While their work is focused more on products, processes, or policies, participants in collegial inquiry focus on deepening their understanding of an issue, problem, or practice through systematic investigation.

THE INQUIRY PROCESS

Collegial inquiry is a disciplined, recursive approach to professional learning with a cycle of behaviors that involves establishing a focus; generating questions; taking action; collecting and analyzing data; reflecting; adjusting course; and, often, generating new questions to pursue.

This reflexive process supports learning and improved practice, and it comprises three stages:

- **Planning** begins with establishing a focus, generating research questions, and envisioning success.
- **Implementation** includes taking action, collecting and analyzing data, reading professional literature, and discussion.
- **Analysis and reflection** often lead a group to cycle back to planning and implementation.

See figure 1 for an illustration of the collegial inquiry process.

Figure 1 | **The Collegial Inquiry Cycle**

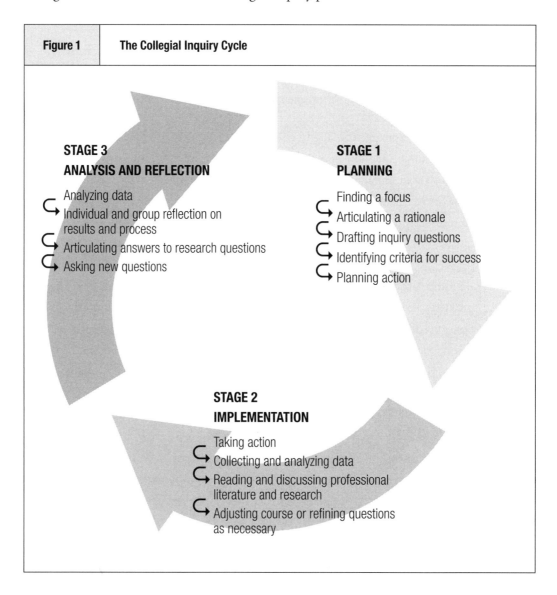

STAGE 3
ANALYSIS AND REFLECTION

- Analyzing data
- Individual and group reflection on results and process
- Articulating answers to research questions
- Asking new questions

STAGE 1
PLANNING

- Finding a focus
- Articulating a rationale
- Drafting inquiry questions
- Identifying criteria for success
- Planning action

STAGE 2
IMPLEMENTATION

- Taking action
- Collecting and analyzing data
- Reading and discussing professional literature and research
- Adjusting course or refining questions as necessary

IMPROVING THE CULTURE OF LEARNING

Collegial inquiry fosters the development of important dispositions that support professional learning communities and contribute to leadership capacity. Educators engaged in collegial inquiry must

- work for deep understanding,
- develop intellectual perseverance,
- commit to reflective practice,
- build a commitment to collaborative and collegial work,
- recognize and honor others' expertise, and
- be courageous.

These dispositions can improve the culture of a learning organization and contribute to sustainable growth (Martin-Kniep, 2007).

Because the process of inquiry includes ongoing questioning, reading, data collection and analysis, and the consideration of multiple perspectives, it requires the educators involved to be committed to building a deep understanding of an issue, problem, or practice. The process also requires intellectual perseverance, because it takes time to learn deeply and ensure true understanding before taking action. Literacy coach Shirley Glickman (personal communication) speaks to these dispositions when she writes:

> As my initial curiosity grew into an abiding interest, and then blossomed into a full-blown passion, I found myself wanting more and more information about what students were thinking, about what teachers were thinking, about the learning itself . . . . Each time I examined new data, the questions bombarded me—Where did the learning go forward? Where did the learning stop (high tide)? Where did it seemingly recede? And of course, the underlying and overriding question, Why?

As Glickman attests, educators engaged in the inquiry process regularly reflect on their understanding and practice as individuals and in groups. They collect and analyze data to make informed and sound decisions, and they engage in individual and collective goal setting and monitoring.

Educators who study deeply together often come to value collegial learning and learn to maximize the various perspectives in a learning community. Because collegial inquiry requires educators to share their thinking, question together, make decisions, and consider one another's perspectives on teaching and learning, over time these members learn to support, respect, and listen to their peers. The various perspectives they bring to the work serve to deepen understanding and improve quality. As one educator said (personal communication):

> Whereas I previously enjoyed collegiality for its own sake, since learning with others can be pleasurable, I now understand that it was not just pleasant but necessary for learning to take place. The irony that I came to this new understanding while engaged in collegial inquiry is not lost on me.

Finally, collegial inquiry empowers individuals and groups to honor and make a commitment to developing expertise and can foster courage and initiative among the members of a learning community. Because the inquiry process is learner-centered, it fosters true ownership of learning. As educators gain confidence and view themselves as professionals able to do research, they often develop the courage to share their learning outside of their inquiry group and even their learning organization. Another educator wrote (personal communication):

> Teachers should be researchers. So much of what we try in our classrooms comes from other teachers. I think we take too much at face value. Becoming researchers ourselves allows us to document what *we* do and why we do it—and to share that with our colleagues.

This belief is at the heart of practical action research. It assumes that practitioners should contribute to the body of research that guides our practice. And it supports the belief that, to balance the rigorous quantitative research that abounds, we need the "stories behind the numbers, the qualitative…to see practical application in a local environment" (Reeves, 2010, p. 72).

While educators engaged in collegial inquiry study together, ask questions about their practice within specific contexts, and reflect, they certainly can change and learn in ways that improve teaching and student learning. The less tangible, but no less important, outcome their study may have is that their developing and changing ways of working may positively affect the learning culture of a building. In this way, collegial inquiry can effect change that is far greater than its initial purpose.

REFERENCES

Martin-Kniep, G. O. (2007). *Communities that learn, lead, and last: Building and sustaining educational expertise.* San Francisco, CA: Jossey-Bass.

Mills, G. E. (2007). *Action research: A guide for the teacher researcher* (3rd ed.). Upper Saddle River, NJ: Prentice Hall.

Reeves, D. (2010). *Transforming professional development into student results.* Alexandria, VA: ASCD.

Richardson, V. (Ed.). (2001). *Handbook of research on teaching* (4th ed.). Washington, DC: American Educational Research Association.

Organization of This Action Tool

This action tool is designed for educators who are new to collegial inquiry or those who are already engaged in the approach and want to improve the processes and rigor of their work. Whether educators are pursuing the same questions together or different questions within an inquiry community, the tools can be helpful.

The sections of this action tool reflect, in part, the critical phases of planning, implementation, and reflection. They are organized so that an inquiry group can use the sections in order or seek out the sections that will best support the inquiry it is already engaged in.

Section 1 is a foundation section that provides tools that can help a group of educators develop a common understanding of the process and can dispel some initial worries about what the process is like.

Sections 2 and 3—which constitute stage 1 of the inquiry cycle—guide the initial planning of the collegial inquiry process and help a group identify a meaningful starting point, think through a rationale and vision for its work, and generate questions to guide the inquiry. Because there is often the need to reexamine focus and capture new questions, the group may revisit these sections as it studies over time.

Sections 4 and 5—which constitute stage 2 of the inquiry cycle—and sections 6 and 7—which constitute stage 3 of the inquiry cycle—support the ongoing work that makes up collegial inquiry: action planning, discourse, the effective use of data, and continuous reflection. You may use them in any order, depending on the needs of your group at particular times in the process.

In addition, each section includes a personal learning journal that can support individual or group reflection on the various aspects of the collegial inquiry process.

Every tool in the collection includes an explanation of why the tool is helpful; process steps for using the tool; and, where helpful, examples of completed tools. Instructional leaders of all sorts—grade-level leaders, department leaders, principals, assistant principals, and staff developers—who are responsible for facilitating collegial inquiry can examine, tailor, and use these tools with groups to improve the collegial inquiry process.

ELECTRONIC TOOLS AND RESOURCES

The tools are available for download. To access these documents, visit www.ascd.org/ downloads and enter the key code found on page vii. All files are saved in Adobe Portable Document Format (PDF). The PDF is compatible with both personal computers (PCs) and Macintosh computers. The main menu will let you navigate through the various sections, and you can print individual tools or sections in their entirety. If you are having difficulties downloading or viewing the files, contact webhelp@ascd.org for assistance, or call 1-800-933-ASCD.

MINIMUM SYSTEM REQUIREMENTS

Program: The most current version of the Adobe Reader software is available for free download at www.adobe.com.

PC: Intel Pentium Processor; Microsoft Windows XP Professional or Home Edition (Service Pack 1 or 2), Windows 2000 (Service Pack 2), Windows XP Tablet PC Edition, Windows Server 2003, or Windows NT (Service Pack 6 or 6a); 128 MB of RAM (256 MB recommended); up to 90 MB of available hard-disk space; Internet Explorer 5.5 (or higher), Netscape 7.1 (or higher), Firefox 1.0, or Mozilla 1.7.

Macintosh: PowerPC G3, G4, or G5 processor, Mac OS X v.10.2.8–10.3; 128 MB of RAM (256 MB recommended); up to 110 MB of available hard-disk space; Safari 1.2.2 browser supported for MAC OS X 10.3 or higher.

GETTING STARTED

Select "Download files." Designate a location on your computer to save the file. Choose to open the PDF file with your existing version of Adobe Acrobat Reader, or install the newest version of Adobe Acrobat Reader from www.adobe.com. From the main menu, select a section by clicking on its title. To view a specific tool, open the Bookmarks tab in the left navigation pane and then click on the title of the tool.

PRINTING TOOLS

To print a single tool, select the tool by clicking on its title via the Bookmarks section and the printer icon, or select File then Print. In the Print Range section, select Current Page to print the page on the screen. To print several tools, enter the page range in the "Pages from" field. If you wish to print all of the tools in the section, select All in the Printer Range section and then click OK.

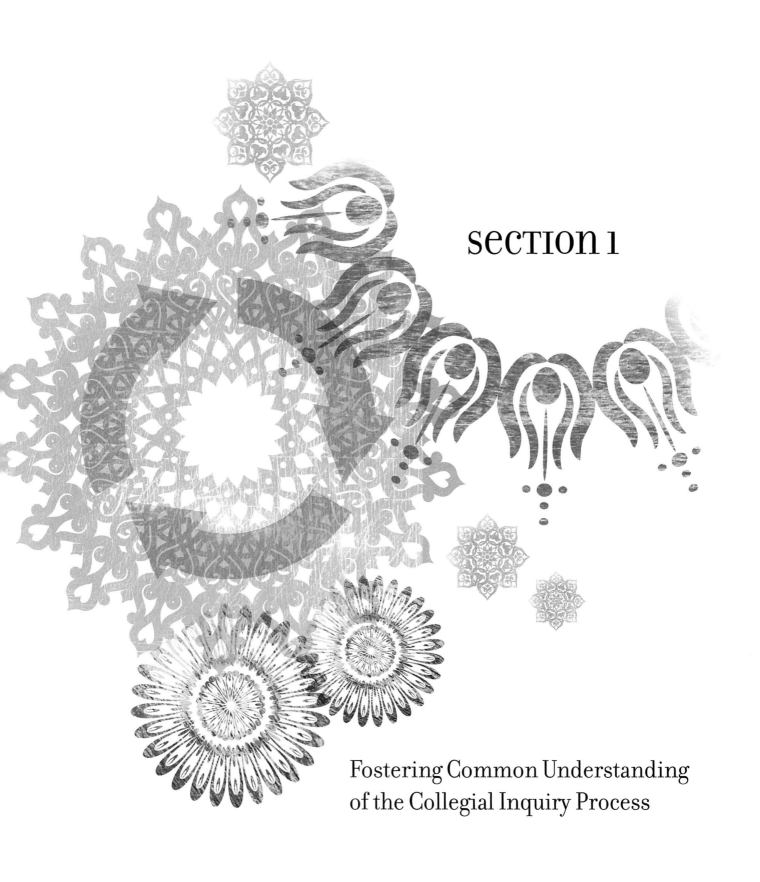

SECTION 1

Fostering Common Understanding
of the Collegial Inquiry Process

SECTION 1

Fostering Common Understanding of the Collegial Inquiry Process

Defining the Characteristics of Collegial Inquiry 16

Assessing the Quality of a Collegial Inquiry Plan.............................. 20

Understanding What Makes Professional Learning Communities Successful.......... 30

Considering Research Validity in Collegial Inquiry.............................. 36

Personal Learning Journal 1... 41

Defining the Characteristics of Collegial Inquiry

There are many definitions of *collegial inquiry* and *action research*, and participants in the inquiry group may have different understandings of and experiences with the process. It is important to uncover your conceptions and assumptions and create a common vision of the process, which will support the group as you begin to create an inquiry plan together.

In this tool, members of the inquiry group examine several descriptions of collegial inquiry and, together, identify similarities among the examples. You then discuss the questions that relate to the work you'll be doing together.

USING THE TOOL

1. Group members divide into pairs or triads and read the three examples of collegial inquiry.

2. As you read, look for similarities among the examples and make a list of aspects they have in common. Jot down any questions you may have.

3. Each pair or triad shares with the whole group what it has noticed about the examples.

4. As a group, create your own definition of *collegial inquiry* that captures the members' understandings of the process, sharing and discussing any questions that arise in the process.

Examples of Collegial Inquiry

EXAMPLE 1

Four administrators, six classroom teachers, and two literacy specialists explore the question, What does quality assessment practice look like in the classroom? They meet one to two times per month for an entire year to identify indicators of quality assessment and draft tools to use with teachers. They consider feedback from others in the school community, read related literature, and revise the tools over time.

This is a long process, but their revisions lead to deeper understanding and improved tools. They also realize the power that multiple perspectives can bring. All year, they regularly reflect on their changing and deepening understanding of the complexity of assessment, both individually and as a group, and record new questions as they emerge. The new questions guide their continued work in years two and three.

EXAMPLE 2

A group of 2nd grade teachers decide to analyze their students' written responses to literature using a literature-response rubric. Over the course of the school year, they analyze samples from select children in the classroom, who represent the range of abilities, in an effort to answer the question, How will students' abilities to respond to literature change over time?

As they work, they realize that their expectations are too low, and they revise their rubric to demand more from students. At the end of the year, they have new questions to explore: How will verbal responses to literature differ from written responses? Will students be more elaborate in their responses or respond differently when they don't have to write? The teachers share their learning with other grade levels and invite others to consider exploring with them in year two.

EXAMPLE 3

A cross-role group of educators from three different education organizations meets every three weeks for one school year to explore the topic of coaching. At the start, they explore such questions as, What is coaching? and How will we define coaching? After defining the term for themselves, they shift to thinking about other questions, such as, How do we engage a resistant learner? How do we come up with the right questions to ask? How do we handle the difficult conversations? and What role does trust play?

To answer these questions for themselves, they read, discuss, interview others about their coaching experiences, and reflect on their practices. Midway through the year, they begin to collaborate on the design of coaching tools and begin to ask questions about new actions they are taking related to the effect these tools have on the coaching experience. They then collect resulting data, explore analysis strategies together, and reflect on new learning.

Defining Collegial Inquiry

My definition of *collegial inquiry:* _____

_____

Similarities Among Examples	My Questions

The group's shared definition of *collegial inquiry:* _____

_____

Assessing the Quality of a Collegial Inquiry Plan

Both before the group begins planning as well as while the group is creating its inquiry plan (see "Planning for Action" on page 94), a checklist for the quality of a plan can be a useful tool. Planning requires deliberate and strategic thinking. In taking time to plan, a group increases its own clarity about the work it is doing and can be sure to meet the standards for high-quality inquiry that support learning.

Before you create an inquiry plan, the checklist and accompanying examples in this tool provide a vision or standard of high quality that can guide your plan. Together, the checklist and examples make the plan more concrete and allow you to discuss and clarify various pieces that should be a part of your plan.

During the design of an inquiry project, you can use the checklist as a self-check or a revision tool, allowing you to reconsider the decisions you are making about your focus, questions, and actions. In addition, you can use the checklist to evaluate and approve plans, such as in cases when teacher centers or nonprofit organizations provide small grants to educators. (For more information about exploratory and action-oriented inquiry, see "Two Types of Inquiry: Exploratory and Action Oriented" on page 72.)

USING THE TOOL

Before Planning

1. Choose one of the sample collegial inquiry plans to read and discuss, or look at both examples.

2. As a group, assess the plan using the criteria in the checklist, discussing and supporting your assessment by referencing the specific plan.

3. Discuss one of the following questions:

   • What have we learned from examining the plan with the checklist?

   • How does this cause us to rethink our image of collegial inquiry?

Assessing the Quality of a Collegial Inquiry Plan

While Planning

1. As a group, review each criterion in the checklist. Look for evidence of that measure in your plan or work and discuss how well your plan meets it.

2. As necessary, refine or revise your work to better align with the criteria in the checklist.

Inquiry Plan Example 1: Grade 1 Collegial Inquiry Group

Selected topic: Helping 1st graders think and talk together about the books they are reading.

RATIONALE

An exploration of how to help 1st graders think and talk together about the books they are reading will benefit students, teachers, and the school community.

Our study has the potential to help students

- Understand that reading is making meaning.
- Improve their ability to learn from written information.
- Improve their ability think about texts at different levels.
- Improve their ability to talk with others to deepen understanding.
- Understand that talking about books and listening to their peers can help them understand what they read.
- Become invested and interested in reading through dialogue.

Our study has the potential to help us

- Meet the needs of all children in our classrooms.
- Deepen our understanding of what deep thinking and high-quality talk look like in 1st grade.
- Improve our questioning strategies and our ability to scaffold questions to bring students to thinking deeply and talking about their reading.
- Increase the level of student engagement in conversations about books.
- Build instructional skills that will transfer to other areas.
- Build assessment skills into the thinking and talking about reading.

Our study has the potential to help other professionals in our school or organization

- Build a foundation for 2nd grade teachers to work from.
- Support and strengthen the initiative in grades 3–5 that is focused on deepening response to literature.

- Support the schoolwide focus on high-quality questioning and conversation.
- Support the goal of building lifelong learners.

Our study can be supported by research from Resnick, Collins, Caulkins, Harvey, Fountas, Pinnell, and Cole.

INQUIRY QUESTIONS

Exploratory Questions

- What are reasonable expectations for 1st graders in terms of sitting and talking about literature?
- What are our students capable of now, in terms of sitting and talking about literature?

Action-Oriented Questions

- How will planning our questions in advance help us support high-quality talk? How will scaffolding our questions lead to deeper thinking?
- How will a unit that establishes routines and structures for book talk support the thinking process?
- How will careful planning partnerships support deep thinking and talk?

ACTION PLANNING

Target Research Questions	Action Items
October 25 Meeting	
• What are reasonable expectations for 1st graders in terms of sitting and talking about literature?	1. We will all have read Chapter 6 of Kathy Collins's *Growing Readers* prior to meeting on October 25. 2. We will have a text-based discussion on Chapter 6 and videotape the discussion. 3. We will create a list of skills and strategies of thinking and talking based on the reading. 4. We will analyze the skills and strategies we used in our discussion and add to the list. (baseline data of our own understanding) 5. Ms. S will arrange for one meeting in early November.

Assessing the Quality of a Collegial Inquiry Plan

Target Research Questions	Action Items
Between October 25 and November 29	
• How will planning our questions in advance help us support accountable talk? How will scaffolding our questions lead to deeper thinking? • What are our students capable of now, in terms of sitting and talking about literature?	1. We will select a text and generate thought-provoking questions to ask students. 2. Each teacher will create a heterogeneous group of students and engage them in a discussion about the text selected. We will videotape five minutes of discussion from each classroom. (baseline data of students' abilities)
November 29 Meeting	
• What are reasonable expectations for 1st graders in terms of sitting and talking about literature?	1. We will view and analyze the videos of our students using the list of thinking and talking skills appropriate for 1st grade. (data analysis) 2. We will continue action planning for the next meetings. 3. We will complete an end-of-session reflection on our learning thus far. (data on our own learning)

CRITERIA FOR RIGOR

☑ The group will read and use current research and thinking on the topic.

☑ The group will access and use multiple perspectives on the topic.

☐ The group members will identify and use pertinent new learning in their practice.

☑ The group members will collect and share evidence (data) of applied learning.

☑ The group will use various types of data over the course of the study.

☑ The group will regularly reflect on learning, application of learning, and group processes.

☐ The group will use protocols to guide discussion, data analysis, and sharing.

☐ The group will document its learning and practice over time.

Source: Used with permission from Shirley Glickman, PS 24, Bronx, N.Y.

Inquiry Plan Example 2:
K–5 Group of Elementary Teachers

Selected topic: Exploring multiple intelligences and learning styles as a way to support our struggling students.

RATIONALE

We are most concerned with our struggling students. We need alternative approaches for small-group instruction, and we also want to get our students to think more and be more involved in the learning process. Also, we believe that we need different ways to assess students, rather than relying on the same forms of assessments. We would like time to extend our learning that began at last year's professional development, and we want an opportunity to work together creatively to meet this classroom challenge.

EXPLORATORY QUESTIONS

1. What are the various learning styles and multiple intelligences?

2. Do we know our own learning styles and intelligences?

3. How do you identify the intelligences of a child?

4. How do you plan lessons and curriculum to incorporate the various learning styles and intelligences?

Assessing the Quality of a Collegial Inquiry Plan

ACTION PLAN

Target Research Questions	Action Items
Prior to November 7	
What are the various learning styles and multiple intelligences?	Meet with your assigned triad and 1. Choose a reading about learning styles and intelligences. 2. Duplicate it for the whole group. 3. Read it and prepare to highlight the important points with the rest of the group at the November meeting. <u>Members of Triads:</u> J, T, A / C, W, G / E, A, L
November 7 Meeting	
Do we know our own learning styles and intelligences?	1. Each member will complete a multiple intelligences inventory. We will discuss our learning based on our profiles. (data on intelligences) 2. Triads report out on readings. 3. Review protocols, which the facilitator will bring, for assessing intelligences.
Prior to December 12	
How do you identify the intelligences of a child?	1. Each member will identify three hard-to-reach students from his or her class and then choose or modify a protocol for assessing the various intelligences. 2. Each member will use a protocol on at least one student and collect samples of student work. (data collection for student intelligences)
December 12 Meeting	
How do you plan lessons and curriculum to incorporate the various learning styles and intelligences?	1. Each member will come with a protocol and samples of work from one student and present a case study to other members. 2. The group will brainstorm strategies to match the intelligences of that child. 3. We will plan for forthcoming meetings and write a request for extended time.

Assessing the Quality of a Collegial Inquiry Plan

CRITERIA FOR RIGOR

- ☑ The group will read and use current research and thinking on the topic.

- ☑ The group will access and use multiple perspectives on the topic.

- ☑ The group members will identify and use pertinent new learning in their practice.

- ☑ The group members will collect and share evidence of applied learning.

- ☑ The group will use various types of data over the course of the study.

- ☑ The group will regularly reflect on learning, application of learning, and group processes.

- ☐ The group will use protocols to guide discussion, data analysis, and sharing.

- ☑ The group will document its learning and practice over time (agenda and discussion notes).

Section 1

Checklist for a High-Quality Collegial Inquiry Plan

FOCUS

☐ Is clear.

☐ Is meaningful for every member of the team.

☐ Is connected to work responsibilities.

☐ Is closely linked to student learning.

RATIONALE

☐ Clearly and specifically makes a case for collaborative study, identifying benefits for students, members of the group, and perhaps even the wider school or district community.

☐ References the group's current knowledge and experiences as well as professional literature that supports the focus.

☐ Explains why the group will take the actions it has selected (if action-oriented inquiry).

☐ Explains why data needs to be collected and analyzed before identifying actions for study (if exploratory inquiry).

ACTIONS (if action-oriented inquiry)

☐ Are specifically described with reference to who is involved and how the actions will be carried out.

QUESTIONS

☐ Are specific and concise.

☐ Reveal the focus and connect to the rationale for the study.

☐ Contain the action being studied (if action-oriented inquiry).

☐ Are phrased so that a yes/no answers are not possible.

☐ Provide guidance for data collection and analysis.

☐ Will take time to explore, will likely uncover various perspectives, and will likely lead to other questions.

Assessing the Quality of a Collegial Inquiry Plan

DATA-COLLECTION TECHNIQUES

☐ Will provide the information needed to answer the research questions.

☐ Include multiple sources and types of data.

☐ Are manageable in terms of types and numbers.

☐ Fit into the group members' work lives and have the possibility of becoming automatic.

ACTION PLANS/MEETING AGENDAS

☐ Include clear action steps for the group's work.

☐ Explicitly connect actions to inquiry questions.

☐ Include group activities as well as individual activities.

☐ Include strategies for documenting the group's learning and changing thinking.

☐ Allow time for reflection by individuals or the group.

Understanding What Makes Professional Learning Communities Successful

Collegial inquiry groups are a type of professional learning community. When groups of educators come together to engage in inquiry, they often have different conceptions of what professional learning communities are, how they operate, and what is essential for success. It's important to give individuals and the group time to think about the factors that contribute to the development of successful professional learning communities and to begin to establish a common vision.

This activity will begin to reveal the conditions and contextual factors that can support the work and will help you later establish group norms or ground rules (see "Establishing Ground Rules" on page 120) for your work. The tool is designed to tap into your current understandings and deepen that understanding through examining excerpts from professional literature.

USING THE TOOL

1. Working individually, take a few minutes to think about the last time you felt like a part of a successful professional learning community, then answer the questions in part 1. If you haven't been involved in a successful learning community, describe an experience when a learning community did not develop.

2. Individuals share in round-robin fashion.

3. As a group, discuss what contributes to the success of a professional learning community.

    • Post ideas on a piece of chart paper or a SMART Board.

    • Present your thinking by writing, listing, drawing, diagramming, or combinations of these.

4. Individually read the five excerpts related to professional learning communities (see pages 33–35), looking for connections to and differences between the readings and the group's previous thinking.

5. As a group, discuss similarities and differences and reviews your initial ideas. Add to or refine your thinking on the chart paper or SMART Board based on the discussion.

What Makes a Successful Professional Learning Community

Section 1

1. INDIVIDUAL REFLECTION

Think about the last time you felt like a part of a successful professional learning community (PLC). (If you've never been part of a successful PLC, consider instead an experience when a learning community did not develop. What was that experience like? What interfered with success?)

- What was that experience like?

- What did you gain from the community?

- What made your experience satisfying?

- What contributed to success?

2. GROUP DISCUSSION

What contributes to the success of a professional learning community?

Understanding What Makes Professional Learning Communities Successful

3. INDIVIDUAL READING

Similarities Between Excerpts and Our Thinking About Successful PLCs	Differences Between Excerpts and Our Thinking About Successful PLCs

Excerpts About Professional Learning Communities

EXCERPT 1

We understand that most learning takes place within an individual but occurs through a process of social interaction that creates conditions for personal transformation. Such change usually happens when a learner is **building community** with other learners who are **constructing knowledge** through their own experience and **supporting learners** involved with them in **documenting reflection** on their experiences and **assessing expectations** agreed on as they are **changing cultures** in their classrooms, institutions, workplaces, or organizations through their own actions. These six essential conditions are necessary for successful professional development experiences because they promote healthy communities of learning.

Source: From *Learning Circles: Creating Conditions for Professional Development* (pp. xiii), by M. Collay, D. Dunlap, W. Enloe, and G. W. Gagnon, 1998, Thousand Oaks, CA: Corwin Press.

EXCERPT 2

We learn with others. Our intelligence is derived from our interactions with others. Our ability to make sense of the realities we face, to interact successfully with our environment, to learn from our experiences, is derived from collaborative and collective problem finding and solving. People who work in schools and whose professional lives are about teaching and learning know much about what works, what does not work, and what could work. They have the wisdom of practice. What they do not have are structured and consistent opportunities dedicated to accessing, further developing and distributing that wisdom....Professional learning communities address our need for affiliation and provide practitioners and other individuals who are committed to schools with structures and processes for sharing social identity, even a cause, and for developing and sharing the wisdom of experience.

Source: From *Communities That Learn, Lead, and Last* (p. xiv), by G. O. Martin-Kniep, 2008, San Francisco, CA: John Wiley and Sons.

EXCERPT 3

Collaborative learning...offers a process for simultaneously promoting individual and organizational capacity building....Collaborative learning assumes a shared focus, a shared responsibility to learn, and a disciplined approach to acquiring the desired goal. It demands that individuals shed the expert role and adopt a collaborative approach that recognizes the values, knowledge, and expertise of all community members.

Source: From *Educators as Learners: Creating a Professional Learning Community in Your School* (p. 4), by P. J. Wald and M. S. Castleberry, 2000, Alexandria, VA: ASCD.

EXCERPT 4

A key feature of productive group work is what Johnson and Johnson (1975) call *positive interdependence*. In fact, positive interdependence is considered by many to be the defining quality and most important component of cooperative group work.

When established successfully, positive interdependence results in students' recognizing that their individual success is inextricably linked to the success of every other member of the group. The realization only occurs when the accomplishment of a group task requires more than just segmenting the work into smaller pieces for members to do alone. The structure of the task must demand that each member of the group offers a unique contribution to the joint effort. When students perceive that every member is indispensible to achieving their mutual goals and that they are both dependent on and obligated to their peers, conditions are ripe for collaborative learning.

Source: From *Productive Group Work* (p. 23), by N. Frey, D. Fischer, and S. Everlove, 2009, Alexandria, VA: ASCD.

EXCERPT 5

10 Essential Elements of Healthy, Inquiry-Oriented PLCs

Healthy, inquiry-oriented PLCs comprise the following elements:

1. Establish a vision that creates momentum for their work.

2. Build trust among group members.

3. Pay attention to the ways power can influence group dynamics.

4. Understand and embrace collaboration.

5. Encourage, recognize, and appreciate diversity within the group.

6. Promote the development of critical friends.

7. Hold the group accountable for and document learning.

Understanding What Makes Professional Learning Communities Successful

8. Understand change and acknowledge the discomfort it may bring to some PLC members.

9. Have a comprehensive view of what constitutes data, and are willing to consider all forms and types of data throughout the PLC work.

10. Work with building administrators.

Source: From *The Reflective Educator's Guide to Professional Development: Coaching Inquiry-Oriented Learning Communities* (pp. 23–47), by N. Fichtman Dana and D. Yendol-Hoppey, 2008, Thousand Oaks, CA: Corwin Press.

Considering Research Validity in Collegial Inquiry

Educators come to the collegial inquiry process with notions of what constitutes valid research and what doesn't. Often their understanding of scientific and objective research gets in the way of understanding the criteria that make collegial inquiry or action research valid.

The rubrics in this tool, which describe four types of validity—democratic, outcome, process, and catalytic—that apply to collegial inquiry and action research, can dispel worries that you may bring and promote reflection during the inquiry process.

Inquiry groups can use this tool at the start of the process as a means of understanding the criteria for validity. During your work, you can use the rubrics as a reflective lens for determining whether your work is valid.

USING THE TOOL

1. As a group, read across the definition for each type of validity. Think about the reflective questions underneath each, and discuss how well your group is addressing that type of validity.

Considering Research Validity in Collegial Inquiry

Rubrics for Validity in Collegial Inquiry

DEMOCRATIC VALIDITY*

Lacks Validity	Approaching Validity	Valid	Highly Valid
Inquiry is done in isolation without taking into account others' perspectives or thinking.	Inquiry relies too exclusively on one perspective.	Inquiry is done collaboratively and uses multiple perspectives from the group and from the research to inform the process.	Inquiry is done collaboratively and uses multiple perspectives to guide the design, implementation, and analysis of data.

Reflective Questions

- How is your group accessing different perspectives?

- What perspectives are most important?

- How are you using perspectives that are different from your own?

Section 1

OUTCOME VALIDITY*

Lacks Validity	Approaching Validity	Valid	Highly Valid
The inquiry is treated as a one-time incident of action and data collection.	The inquiry spiral is incomplete: the group's actions did not lead to answers, and the group did not attempt to redirect the inquiry so that it could be meaningful.	The inquiry reveals a successful completion of the inquiry spiral: the group's work either leads to answers or to a reframing of the inquiry with new questions.	The inquiry reveals a successful completion of the inquiry spiral: the group's actions lead to answers and naturally guide the group to new research questions that would extend and deepen their understanding.

Reflective Questions

- How is the group handling new questions that arise?

- When the group feels it has answers, is there a reframing with new questions? Why or why not?

Considering Research Validity in Collegial Inquiry

PROCESS VALIDITY*

Lacks Validity	Approaching Validity	Valid	Highly Valid
The group uses a simplistic and biased approach to data collection and analysis that would make conclusions highly questionable.	The group uses a biased approach to data collection through limited sources or reliance on one perspective, which raises questions about the meaning and value of conclusions.	The group uses multiple sources of data to support and draw conclusions that are meaningful.	The group uses multiple sources and types of data to support and make conclusions that are credible and meaningful.

Reflective Questions

- What data sources are being used?

- Do the data sources represent different perspectives?

- Do data sources vary in type and form?

CATALYTIC VALIDITY*

Lacks Validity	Approaching Validity	Valid	Highly Valid
The inquiry does not seem to result in any change in thinking or practice for the group.	The inquiry has confirmed the group's thinking and has led to minor changes in practice.	The inquiry has deepened the group's understanding about the topic and has led to important changes in practice.	The inquiry has deepened the group's understanding about the topic, has transformed practice in significant ways, and has led to adjustments in philosophy.

Reflective Questions

- How is your thinking changing?

- What changes in practice have resulted from the inquiry? How significant are these changes?

- How has the work reoriented you or transformed you?

*Validity definitions summarized from *Studying Your Own School: An Educator's Guide to Practitioner Action Research* (pp. 147–154), by G. L. Anderson, K. Herr, and A. S. Nihlen, 2007, Thousand Oaks, CA: Corwin Press.

Personal Learning Journal 1

A personal learning journal allows individual group members to reflect on their own deepening understanding of the work they are engaged in. The journal is a quiet space for you to clarify, question, and think about your learning and participation in the group.

The journal can be a private thinking tool or, if individuals share after writing, a jumping-off point for group reflection. The journal can be on paper or posted to an online discussion board so that group members can see and respond to one another's thinking.

USING THE TOOL

1. The facilitator of the group meeting (see "Facilitating Collegial Inquiry" on page 122) provides the questions to members of the group and explains that they may respond to all or some of the questions.

   • If you use the journal during a group meeting, provide enough time for thoughtful response.

2. (Optional) Allow for the sharing of individual reflection at the end of a meeting, at the start of a meeting, or between sessions via a discussion board, Google Group, or electronic mailing list.

ASCD   41

Personal Learning Journal for Section 1

1. How has my understanding of collegial inquiry changed?

2. What did I learn about inquiry from examining examples?

3. How has my group's conversation about inquiry and professional learning communities contributed to my deepening understanding?

4. What did I learn about the group I am working with?

5. What am I wondering now?

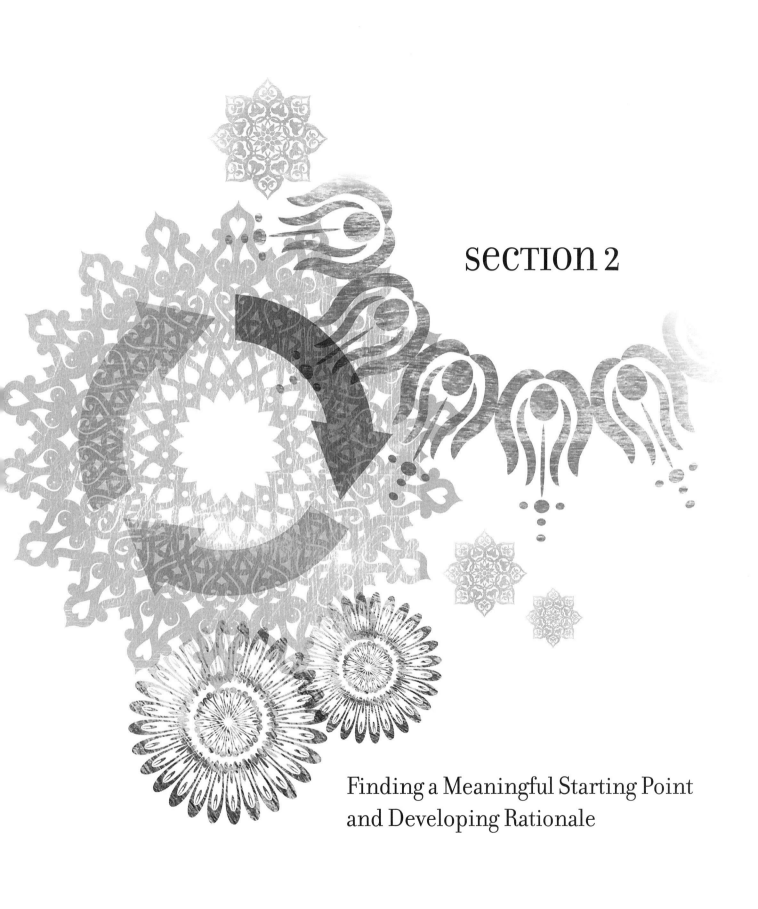

section 2

Finding a Meaningful Starting Point
and Developing Rationale

SECTION 2

Finding a Meaningful Starting Point and Developing Rationale

Identifying Inquiry Topics 46

Selecting a Topic 48

Ensuring a Meaningful Starting Point 50

Developing a Rationale 54

Assessing the Quality of Your Rationale 60

Creating a Vision for Success 62

Personal Learning Journal 2 66

Identifying Inquiry Topics

Collegial inquiry starts with identifying a topic or focus. A meaningful focus for inquiry is sustainable over time—that is, it may continue beyond a single academic year and could continue with different members—and is supported by both the members of the inquiry group and the school or district.

Although you can take into consideration the roles, struggles, and passions of the group members, you need to look at the bigger picture to ensure that inquiry is linked to the learning priorities of the school or district community. This tool provides guiding questions for brainstorming possible topics for study.

USING THE TOOL

1. Choose a facilitator (see "Facilitating Collegial Inquiry" on page 122), who then poses the questions on page 47 to the group by posting them on a chart, an overhead, or a whiteboard. Each of these starting points is slightly different but connected to the learning organization.

2. The group chooses the question that best meets its needs or interests. You also have the option of brainstorming around multiple questions.

3. Identify a timekeeper for the brainstorming session; this could be the facilitator. Limit the brainstorm to 3–5 minutes.

4. Brainstorm, encouraging participants to

    • Share ideas in a round-robin fashion.

    • Mention any idea that comes to mind, even if it seems wild.

    • Withhold making judgments or negative comments about any idea.

    • Focus on the quantity of ideas.

5. Sort the list of ideas by clustering like items and eliminating those that you do not want to pursue. This may take some time, but the discussion is an important step toward finding a meaningful starting point.

Guiding Questions for Identifying Inquiry Topics

1. What are the schoolwide or districtwide goals linked to student learning that may guide the selection of a focus for our study?

2. What professional learning goals has our school or district already established that our study could link to?

3. What professional learning needs do we have related to curriculum, instruction, assessment, or leadership?

4. What are the most urgent needs of our student population? How might we link a study to those needs?

Selecting a Topic

Once the group has brainstormed possible topics for study, you must come to a consensus about the focus of your work. When you are considering several possibilities that seem worthy of your time, the criteria in this tool can provide a lens for examining each possibility carefully and allow you to clarify the topics you are considering.

The criteria emphasize the need to focus on student learning and the importance of using student work to inform practice, a central aspect of disciplined collegial inquiry. They also highlight the importance of choosing a topic that will not only lead to learning and improved practice, but that will also be enhanced by collaboration and multiple perspectives. Finally, the criteria reinforce the idea that the group's work should link to the organization's priorities and ultimately lead to learning and improvement in other related areas.

USING THE TOOL

1. List the topics that the group is considering for inquiry on the lines provided.

2. For each topic, discuss its value and provide a score of 1 (low) to 3 (high) next to each criterion.

3. Select the topic or focus that scores most strongly against the set of criteria.

Scoring Inquiry Topics

Topic A: _____

Topic B: _____

Topic C: _____

Topic D: _____

Rate each criterion as 1(low), 2 (moderate), or 3 (high).

Criteria	Topic A	Topic B	Topic C	Topic D
The topic is closely connected to identified student needs. School and classroom data related to student learning support the need for attention here.				
The topic will result in improved educator knowledge, skills, and efficacy. Each member of the inquiry team can benefit from studying this.				
The topic is job-embedded and will allow for applied practice and collection of data by all members of the inquiry team, even though the application and data collection may be in different settings.				
The topic links directly to explicit schoolwide or districtwide goals.				
The topic is ideal for collaborative inquiry: it is complex and demands the consideration of multiple perspectives.				
The topic is one that the group is ready to tackle because of current knowledge or previous foundational work or specific roles that members hold.				
The topic is one that could have a synergistic effect on other efforts, thereby increasing learning and growth in other areas.				

Ensuring a Meaningful Starting Point

The success of collegial inquiry depends on choosing a meaningful starting point. The focus of the study needs to be meaningful for each individual, the group as a whole, students, and the school community.

By discussing each dimension in the rubric in this tool, you can assess the strength of the topic under consideration.

USING THE TOOL

1. As a group, read across the first dimension of the rubric and circle where you think your topic falls for each criterion.

    *   If you believe the topic exhibits the criterion listed, you should be able to provide an example of an outcome that would support the dimension. (See the example row in the rubric.)
    *   If you struggle to identify a specific example, then you may need to move your assessment down one level.

2. Based on the level of quality of your focus, refine the topic, if necessary, and then reassess.

Ensuring a Meaningful Starting Point

Rubric for Assessing Your Choice of Topic

Dimension	Disconnected	Promising	Meaningful	Meaningful and Systemic
Connection to teaching and student learning (urgency, priority)	• Unconnected to teaching practice, leadership, or student learning.	• Connected, in general, to teaching practice or leading. • Connected to student learning in general or by implication.	• Connected to a specific aspect of teaching practice or leadership that is likely to improve practice. • Connected explicitly to specific student learning.	• Connected to a specific and critical aspect of teaching practice or leadership that will improve practice. • Connected specifically to identified student learning needs and important learning targets that cross disciplinary boundaries.
	Example **Topic:** Reading comprehension strategies **Outcome:** Students will improve in reading.	*Example* **Topic:** Using think-alouds to model reading comprehension strategies **Outcome:** Students will improve in reading comprehension and be able to practice those strategies in their own reading.	*Example* **Topic:** Using think-alouds to model reading comprehension strategies **Outcome:** Students will be able to "see" otherwise invisible strategies that good readers use and will be able to practice those strategies in their own reading.	*Example* **Topic:** Using think-alouds to model reading comprehension strategies **Outcome:** Students will be able to "see" otherwise invisible strategies that good readers use and will be able to practice those strategies in their own reading across all content. This can foster metacognitive thinking that can serve them in many areas.

Ensuring a Meaningful Starting Point

Dimension	Disconnected	Promising	Meaningful	Meaningful and Systemic
Connection to school or district goals (synergy and thinking systemically)	• Unconnected to school or district goals. • Could be considered a distraction from the work of the organization.	• Tangentially linked to school or district goals. • The value of focusing on this is questionable; there may be more important things to focus on.	• Clearly and explicitly connected to school or district goals. • Would support, rather than add to, the work and learning that needs to be done in the school or district.	• Clearly and explicitly connected to school or district goals. • Would support the work and learning that needs to be done. • Could benefit the wider system by informing others' learning and practice.
Meaningfulness to all involved (commitment)	• A few members of the group see the value of the focus in terms of their own practice. • Others members do not see the value and would not commit to an in-depth or sustained study.	• One or more members of the group see the value of the focus in terms of their own practice. • One or more members may be struggling to see the meaningfulness in terms of their own learning or practice. • The focus would need to be modified in some way for all members to commit to a sustained and ongoing study.	• All members in the group find meaningful connections to their learning and practice and can commit to a sustained and ongoing study.	• All members in the group find meaningful connections to their learning and practice. • Everyone is passionate about committing to a sustained and ongoing study.

Ensuring a Meaningful Starting Point

Dimension	Disconnected	Promising	Meaningful	Meaningful and Systemic
Readiness of group to study (prior knowledge, time)	• The group is not ready to tackle the focus. • Prior knowledge is lacking or the focus represents an area that does not allow for individual or group action or application.	• One or more members are ready to tackle the focus, but others struggle in terms of its perceived relevance or meaning to their work.	• The experiences and knowledge of the group have been considered in selection. • The focus provides a good starting point for increasing the group's current knowledge and skills.	• Everyone is ready and committed to the focus of the study. • Members see the focus as intrinsically related to their work and to their increased effectiveness as practitioners and as members of the school system.

53

Developing a Rationale

In designing an inquiry project, you must be clear about your reasons for selecting a focus. Considering the essential question, Why are we doing this? supports deliberate and thoughtful action that prevents a group from rushing to a decision about its work.

Articulating a rationale forces you to consider the various reasons for studying the topic you selected and to justify the expenditure of time and effort necessary to engage in the work. Through the process of defining a rationale, you will also be more prepared to develop focused research questions and identify specific actions to take and data to collect.

As the inquiry group continues planning, you will typically need to revisit and redraft the rationale as the whys of the research become clearer.

USING THE TOOL

1. Group members divide into pairs or triads, and each thoughtfully responds to a different set of one or two questions on "Guiding Questions for Developing a Rationale." It is OK to make a bulleted list to start.

2. The pairs or triads share their thinking for their selected questions, which together form a first draft of the rationale.

3. See the example rationales from other schools' inquiry groups for an idea of what yours may look like.

Guiding Questions for Developing a Rationale

1. How will students benefit as a result of this study?

2. How will inquiry group members benefit? What knowledge will we gain? What skills or abilities can we develop? What dispositions will the study foster?

3. How might our school benefit? Which schoolwide goals or initiatives would the study support or enhance?

4. How might our district benefit? Which districtwide goals or initiatives would the study support or enhance?

5. What current professional literature and research do we know of that supports the study of this topic?

Example Rationale 1

Topic: Helping 1st graders think and talk together about the books they are reading.

RATIONALE

Our study has the potential to help students

- Understand that reading is making meaning.

- Improve their ability to learn from written information.

- Improve their ability think about texts at different levels.

- Improve their ability to talk with others to deepen understanding.

- Understand that talking about books and listening to their peers can help them understand what they read.

- Become invested and interested in reading through dialogue.

Our study has the potential to help us

- Meet the needs of all children in our classrooms.

- Deepen our understanding of what deep thinking and high-quality talk look like in 1st grade.

- Improve our questioning strategies and our ability to scaffold questions to bring students to thinking deeply and talking about their reading.

- Increase the level of student engagement in conversations about books.

- Build instructional skills that will transfer to other areas.

- Build assessment skills into the thinking and talking about reading.

Our study has the potential to help other professionals in our school or organization

- Build a foundation for 2nd grade teachers to work from.

- Support and strengthen the initiative in grades 3–5 that is focused on deepening response to literature.

- Support the schoolwide focus on high-quality questioning and conversation.

- Support the goal of building lifelong learners.

Our study can be supported by research from Resnick, Collins, Caulkins, Harvey, Fountas, Pinnell, and Cole.

Source: Used with permission from Shirley Glickman, PS 24, Bronx, N.Y.

Section 2

57

Example Rationale 2

Topic: Action research as professional development

RATIONALE

The Byram Hills School District is currently participating in a classroom action research course through the Northern Westchester Board of Cooperative Educational Services. Nine teachers and two administrators are participating in the course, and participants will design an action research project for the year.

Participation in this course is supported by the Byram Hills Evaluation Committee and is part of the teacher evaluation cycle for tenured teachers. Teachers currently have the opportunity to participate in a growth plan through the Evaluation Committee; the action research course is a pilot program to provide a structured approach to teacher-centered professional growth.

As administrators and evaluators of teachers, we are interested in how classroom action research enhances teachers' practices that lead to improved student learning. We intend to learn the value of action research as a professional growth opportunity. Therefore, it is imperative to understand (1) the role of the administrator in supporting this work and (2) how classroom action research enhances teachers' knowledge and improves instructional practices.

The literature on school improvement suggests that learning occurs best when done in collaboration with teachers and administrators. For example, one study suggests the following: "Teachers rate learning from other teachers second only to their own teaching experiences as the most valuable source of information about effective teaching".[1] Furthermore, the literature on reform efforts and school improvement suggests that improvements in teacher behaviors endure over time when teachers have input into their professional development.

Our experience informs this work as well. The Byram Hills School District has engaged in a structure for professional learning communities for the past 11 years. Our reflection and

---

[1] Barkley, S. G. [with Bianco, T. (Ed.)]. *Quality teaching in a culture of coaching* (p. 9). Lanham, MD: ScarecrowEducation.

evaluation of the professional learning communities has resulted in increased collegiality and collaboration, improved instructional practices, and ongoing teacher learning. We have learned that to achieve and maintain these results, the administration must (1) provide a structure and allot time for professional learning, (2) provide resources and support, and (3) build capacity for teacher leaders.

Source: Used with permission from Tim Kaltenecker and Carol Fisher, Byram Hills School District, Armonk, N.Y.

Assessing the Quality of Your Rationale

A high-quality rationale speaks to the value of the inquiry for students, the inquiry team, and the wider community. It also references what you know about current professional literature related to the topic you have chosen and the resources you will access to inform your inquiry. For teams that must request support or get approval for their study, a well-articulated rationale is invaluable.

The following rubric for a high-quality rationale can be a self-assessment tool, a facilitator tool (see "Facilitating Collegial Inquiry" on page 122) for providing feedback, or a tool to guide revision of an existing rationale. It is often necessary for a group to come back to the rationale more than once to be sure that it captures all the thinking of group members.

USING THE TOOL

1. Working in pairs, review one of the rationale examples on pages 56–59. Decide where the example rationale falls on the rubric.

2. Discuss the strengths of the rationale, and identify how it might be developed further.

3. When the group is comfortable with the rubric, use it to assess your own rationale draft.

4. Identify your next steps based on your self-assessment. If you rate your rationale as "emerging" or "undeveloped," review the guiding questions on page 55 and revise your rationale.

Assessing the Quality of Your Rationale

Rubric for Rationale Quality

Undeveloped	Emerging	Developed	Exemplary
• Justification is unclear, trivial, or undeveloped. • Support references relevant personal experiences without reference to professional literature or research.	• Justification is implied and unconvincing, because there are only vague references to benefits for students, educators, or the school community. • Support generally references personal experiences, professional literature, or research.	• Justification is specific and explicit, referencing knowledge and skills that both students and educators may develop. • Support includes both general and specific references to personal experiences, professional literature, and research.	• Justification is specific, detailed, and explicit, referencing knowledge, skills, and dispositions that both students and educators may develop. • Justification includes a description of how the school or district community may benefit from the study. • Support includes specific and detailed references to personal experiences, current professional literature, and research.

Creating a Vision for Success

Once a group has identified a focus and articulated a rationale, it can define its criteria for success. Essentially, this process requires you to imagine where, ideally, you will be at the end of one or more years of inquiry. Establishing criteria for success provides a vision and often helps a group further think through and articulate its rationale for study.

When you agree on specific criteria for success, the measures can serve as a tool for ongoing assessment and self-monitoring by both individual members and the entire group. The process of establishing criteria for success can contribute to your determining a course of action and what data will be helpful, reflecting on your work, and evaluating progress—throughout the process.

The questions in this tool lead you to consider your study's various levels of influence, including on your emotions, knowledge, and changing practice and results or effects on learners and the wider professional community.[1] You can also choose to generate criteria related to the collegial inquiry and group learning processes.

Answering the question, How can we assess whether we meet these criteria? or What evidence will show that we have met these criteria? will help guide the group in systematically collecting data and self-assessing.

USING THE TOOL

1. As a group, discuss each guiding question.
2. Identify 2–4 indicators that you believe will evidence your success.
3. Think about each criteria set, and discuss how you might assess and document that success over time.

[1] Guskey, T. R. (2000). *Evaluating professional development.* Thousand Oaks, CA: Corwin Press.

Defining Criteria for Success

Type of Influence	Guiding Questions	Assessment and Documentation (How might we assess and document this? Or where might we see evidence of this?)
Emotions How will we feel about our learning related to our focus?	• • •	
Knowledge and Understanding What new knowledge will we have, or what will we understand more deeply?	• • •	
Changing Practice How will our practice have changed? Or what new skills and abilities will we have developed? Or what will we be able to do that we cannot do now?	• • •	
Results (related to our work with learners) How will our learning affect the learners (students or adults) we work with?	• • •	
Professional Community (outside of this group) How will our learning from this study influence our interactions with others in the school community?	• • •	

Creating a Vision for Success

Example Criteria for Success

The following criteria for success came from a group of 6–8 educators studying their questioning practices. Their rationale for examining this topic came from a schoolwide presentation at a staff development day about quality questioning practices. Their questions included the following:

1. What kinds of questions are we currently asking?
2. What are our own strengths and weaknesses in terms of our questioning practices?
3. How do we plan lessons, tasks, and projects using what we learn about questioning?

Type of Influence	Criteria for Success	Assessment and Documentation (How might we assess and document this? Or where might we see evidence of this?)
Emotions How will we feel about our learning?	• We will feel satisfied and be able to justify (to ourselves) that the time out of the classroom to learn was worthwhile. • We will feel so satisfied that we will be determined to continue the work next year with other colleagues.	• end-of-year reflection and conversation • request to principal for time next year to continue the study
Knowledge and Understanding What new knowledge will we have, or what will we understand more deeply?	• We will understand the various types of questions and be able to identify them, name them, and explain them to our colleagues and to our students in kid-friendly ways. • We will know the definition of wait time and recognize when wait time needs improvement. • We will know what resources exist for quality questioning practices.	• facilitator notes from conversations • examples of lessons and tasks with the questions labeled by type • examples of curriculum units with the questions labeled by type • notes about wait time from our intervisitation with one another • bibliography that we create as we go along

Type of Influence	Criteria for Success	Assessment and Documentation (How might we assess and document this? Or where might we see evidence of this?)
Changing Practice How will our practice have changed? Or what new skills and abilities will we have developed? Or what will we be able to do that we cannot do now?	• We will be able to use various lenses to develop different types of questions. • We will be able to design new lessons and tasks that embed different kinds of questions.	• before-and-after lessons or tasks that show our use of questions • student work samples from the new lessons or tasks that show their responses to questions
Results (related to our work with learners) How will our learning affect the students we work with?	• Our students will be able to identify the types of questions they are responding to and the kind of thinking they demand. • Our students will be able to ask different kinds of questions during discussions and classroom activities. • We will see increased student responses to questions, longer responses, and more thoughtful responses when we improve our wait time.	• observation notes from inter-visitations noting the questions students ask • anecdotal notes about classroom discussions and questions posed • photos of question walls in our classrooms
Professional Community (outside of this group) How will our learning from this study influence our interactions with others in the school community?	• Other teachers will be aware that we are studying questioning practices. • We will informally be sharing our learning when we work together on common assessments and projects that contain questions.	• informal inquiries • common assessments and projects

Section 2

Personal Learning Journal 2

A personal learning journal allows individual group members to reflect on their own deepening understanding of the work they are engaged in. The journal is a quiet space for you to clarify, question, and think about the connection of the work to your learning and practice. The questions also provide you with an opportunity to reflect on the value of writing a rationale and identifying criteria for success and the effect that might have on clarifying, questioning, and thinking further about the group's work.

The journal can be a private thinking tool or, if individuals share after writing, a jumping-off point for group reflection. The journal can be on paper or posted to an online discussion board so that group members can see and respond to one another's thinking.

USING THE TOOL

1. The facilitator of the group meeting (see "Facilitating Collegial Inquiry" on page 122) provides the questions to members of the group and explains that they may respond to all or some of the questions.

    • If you use the journal during a meeting, provide enough time for thoughtful response.

2. (Optional) Allow for the sharing of individual reflection at the end of a meeting; at the start of a meeting; or between sessions via a discussion board, Google Group, or electronic mailing list.

Personal Learning Journal for Section 2

GROUP FOCUS

1. How do I feel about the focus of my group's inquiry?

2. What specific connections can I see to my practice and the learners I work with? What connections can I see to the school community?

3. What reservations do I have about this study, if any?

4. Based on my group's work to come to consensus, what are my thoughts about my group's commitment to the work?

RATIONALE

1. How did writing a rationale help the group clarify our thinking?

2. What was the value of identifying specific criteria for success? How did it cause me to think about my success differently?

3. What questions, if any, emerged from drafting a rationale or identifying criteria for success?

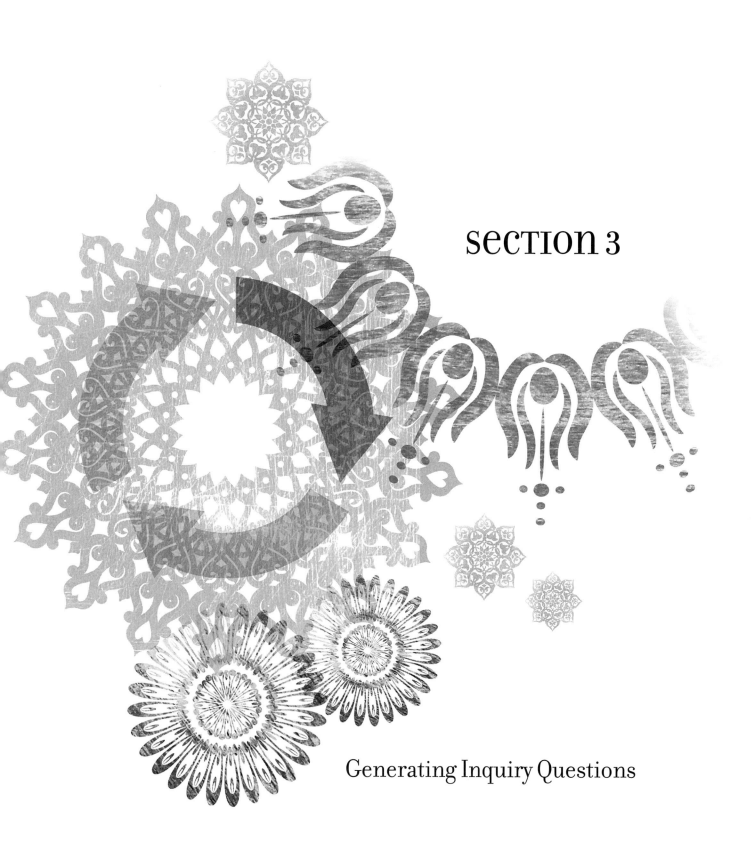

SECTION 3

Generating Inquiry Questions

SECTION 3

Generating Inquiry Questions

Two Types of Inquiry: Exploratory and Action Oriented 72

Crafting Inquiry Questions.. 76

Designing Inquiry Questions from Stems 80

Assessing the Quality of Inquiry Questions................................. 84

Personal Learning Journal 3... 88

Section 3

Two Types of Inquiry: Exploratory and Action Oriented

Depending on the group's experience with and existing depth of knowledge about the selected topic, you may engage in *exploratory inquiry* or in *action-oriented inquiry*. The difference between these two approaches is the stage at which you collect and analyze data.[1]

In exploratory inquiry, also known as *responsive inquiry*, your inquiry involves gathering data about a topic or situation or reading about research-based practices so that you can better understand a situation, approach, or strategy.[1] You can then use your deeper understanding and new information to form your action plan.

Some examples of exploratory questions are

- What kinds of critical thinking skills are my students capable of, and which skills do they struggle with?
- What is critical thinking?

Groups that don't have extensive experience with or knowledge about the topic of the inquiry will most likely use an exploratory approach to inquiry.

In action-oriented inquiry, also known as *proactive inquiry*, you start with a specific action or strategy group members want to use or are already using and form questions based on your knowledge of or experience with it.[1] You then collect data based on the questions you form and revise your practice based on the results.

Some examples of action-oriented questions are

- What will I learn about students' understanding of the content covered in class through the use of science logs?
- How will the job-embedded performance evaluation process (goal-setting portfolio) work with teachers new to my building?

[1] Schmuck, R. A. (1997). *Practical action research for change*. Arlington Heights, IL: Skylight Publishing.

Notice that these two questions embed a specific strategy or action (i.e., use of science logs, use of goal-setting portfolios), which makes them action-oriented.

Distinguishing between these types of questions will support you in deciding how to begin your inquiry, determining what action items to include in meeting agendas, identifying the perspectives you will need in the study, identifying the data you will collect and use for your learning, and generating researchable questions.

USING THE TOOL

1. Review the descriptions and examples of exploratory and action-oriented questions.
2. To further familiarize yourself with the types of inquiry, label the research questions provided as exploratory or action oriented.

Inquiry Question Typology

Exploratory (Responsive) Inquiry Questions	Action-Oriented (Proactive) Inquiry Questions
• Researchers are seeking information so that they can eventually take action. • Researchers read, gather information, and collect and analyze data before taking new actions.	• Researchers are ready to take action or use specific strategies and investigate the results. • Researchers collect and analyze data resulting from their action.
Examples • What kinds of critical-thinking skills are my students capable of? Which skills do they struggle with? • What is critical thinking?	*Examples* • What will we learn about students' understanding of the content through the use of science logs? • How will goal-setting portfolios work with teachers new to the building?

Research Question	Exploratory (no action is explicit in the question)	Action Oriented (reveals an action being taken and studied)
1. What characteristics of a school foster risk taking?		
2. How can we use drama in the content areas to enhance and deepen students' understanding of a text?		
3. What is the role of the library media specialist?		

Two Types of Inquiry: Exploratory and Action Oriented

Research Question	Exploratory (no action is explicit in the question)	Action Oriented (reveals an action being taken and studied)
4. What are the alternatives to the formal observation process?		
5. How can using flexible groups to teach specific skills improve students' ability to read nonfiction?		

Section 3

Crafting Inquiry Questions

Educators engaged in collegial inquiry often want to begin action planning by answering the question, What will we do? The better approach is to answer the question, What questions do we want to answer? Researchers begin with hypotheses to test or questions to answer; it makes sense to begin the collegial inquiry process in the same place.

The focus on questions keeps the spotlight on the learning of the group, rather than on products. Focus questions should

- Emphasize that learning and deepening understanding are most important.
- Serve to identify the best starting points for action.
- Set out a path for study that is responsive to the knowledge and experience of the individuals in the group.
- Provide indicators for success.
- Be used as formative and summative assessment measures for the work.

The process of brainstorming and deciding on specific inquiry questions may take some time, but the conversation is important because it will help you clarify your focus even further and reveal each member's comfort level and experience with the topic. Before beginning to brainstorm questions, revisit your rationale for the inquiry (see "Developing a Rationale" on page 54).

For another approach to formulating focus questions, see "Designing Inquiry Questions from Stems" on page 80.

USING THE TOOL

1. As a group, brainstorm responses to the guiding questions for 3–5 minutes. Write down all questions that come to mind.
2. Review the list, eliminating redundant and unimportant questions.

Crafting Inquiry Questions

3. Group the remaining questions into like clusters. (See page 79 for an example of question clusters.)

4. Prioritize the question clusters, ordering them from most important to least important—or in the way that makes the most sense to the group.

Section 3

Brainstorming and Prioritizing Inquiry Questions

1. Brainstorm responses to the following questions:

   • What questions do we have about our topic or focus?

   • What do we need to know that we don't know?

2. Review the brainstormed list for overlap and connections. Cross out redundant questions.

3. Create question clusters by putting related questions together, combining and revising questions as necessary. Place the clusters in the boxes below, adding more boxes if necessary.

Cluster 1	Cluster 2
Cluster 3	Cluster 4

4. Discuss which questions are most important to the group.

Example of a Question Cluster: 21st Century Skills

As shown below, this inquiry group clustered its questions about 21st century skills into three sets: defining the skills, analyzing them, and thinking about how they will be embedded in schools. They decided to tackle them in the order listed.

DEFINING

- What are the 21st century skills?
- Where did the label "21st century" come from?
- Who defined them?

ANALYZING

- How are they different from or similar to other sets of standards?
- What do they demand of students?
- How are they relevant and meaningful for students?

EMBEDDING

- How will the new set of skills impact teacher practice?
- What are the best curriculum and assessment entry points for addressing them?
- What changes would schools have to make to incorporate them?

Designing Inquiry Questions from Stems

Inquiry questions are the keystone of the inquiry process, and they need to focus on the topic of investigation and be specific enough to guide next steps, actions or interventions, and data collection. Whether for exploratory or action-oriented inquiry (see "Two Types of Inquiry: Exploratory and Action Oriented" on page 72), devising questions that meet these standards is sometimes challenging.

This tool can help you design and refine your inquiry questions by starting with question stems, which can help ensure that your questions emphasize learning, identify the best starting point for action, set a path for study based on existing knowledge, provide indicators for success, and can be used as assessment measures.

For example, consider the action-oriented stem, "What will happen when _____ is _____?" in relation to a focus on book clubs. One possible question would be, "What will happen to student interest in reading when the reading program is supported by book clubs?" The question indicates that researchers are specifically interested in increasing the level of student interest and that they will need to collect data about interest level. This means that the researchers may need to find or create an interest survey so that they can document student interest. If they were also interested in students' vocabulary development, they would have another question and select the appropriate data to document that.

For another approach to formulating focus questions, see "Crafting Inquiry Questions" on page 76.

USING THE TOOL

1. Decide if the group's inquiry is exploratory or action oriented so that you can start with the most useful stems.

2. As a group, generate possible questions using the stems.

3. Refine the questions until all group members are satisfied. (To assess the specificity of your questions, see "Assessing the Quality of Inquiry Questions" on page 84.)

Using Inquiry Question Stems

Topic:

Exploratory Stem	Example	Your Possible Questions
Why does. . .	*Why does the ability to revise pose such a challenge for our students?*	
What is/are. . .	*What is differentiated instruction, exactly?*	
What can we learn from. . .	*What can we learn from examining the science curriculum across grades at the middle school level?*	
Which students are. . .	*Which students are most at risk for not succeeding in math?*	

Designing Inquiry Questions from Stems

Exploratory Stem	Example	Your Possible Questions
What types of learners. . .	*What types of learners are having the most success on our periodic assessments? Why?*	
What approaches might. . .	*What coaching approaches might be effective with first-year teachers?*	
What does the research say about. . .	*What does the research say about the kind of support that first-year teachers need?*	

Action-Oriented Stem	Example	Your Possible Questions
How will the use of _____ affect _____ ?	*How will the use of flexible grouping affect the support of my English language learners' skill development?*	
How does _____ work in ___?	*How does using a discussion board inside of a long-term professional development program work in support of learning?*	

Designing Inquiry Questions from Stems

Action-Oriented Stem	Example	Your Possible Questions
What will happen if we try. . . ?	*What will happen if we try having students peer review prior to the teacher reviewing student proposal drafts?*	
What will happen when _____ is _____?	*What will happen to student interest in reading when the reading program is supported by book clubs?*	
What will we learn about _____ from the use of _____ in _____?	*What will we learn about coaches' effectiveness from the use of a Google Group in the context of a reflective coaching model?*	

Section 3

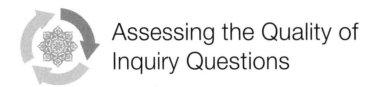

Assessing the Quality of Inquiry Questions

The process of generating precise and specific inquiry questions takes time and revision. The checklist and rubric in this tool will help you assess your questions so that they best guide the inquiry that will follow. You can use this tool in pairs, small groups, or with the entire inquiry team.

USING THE TOOL

1. Read the checklist criteria.

2. For each criterion in the checklist, identify the part of your question that meets that measure.

3. Revise the inquiry question so that it meets most, if not all, of the criteria.

4. Once you've revised your inquiry question, decide where it falls on the quality rubric.

5. If your question isn't of the highest quality, discuss how you might revise it further.

Checklist for High-Quality Inquiry Questions

The inquiry questions

☐ Are clearly connected to the focus of the study.

☐ Reveal the action being taken (if the group is engaged in action-oriented inquiry).

☐ Reveal the rationale for taking action (if the group is engaged in action-oriented inquiry).

☐ Are specific enough to guide action planning.

☐ Are specific enough to guide data collection.

☐ Are specific enough to provide structure for data analysis.

☐ May be used before and after as formative or summative assessment measures of individual and group learning.

Section 3

Rubric for Inquiry Question Quality

Overly General	Combination of General and Specific	Specific and Focused	Highly Specific and Focused
• Research question is related to the focus but is too broad to guide action planning or research.	• Research questions are both broad and specific and are relevant to the focus. • They provide a starting point for action planning but are not explicitly connected to the rationale for the study.	• Research questions are specific, essential to the study, and connected to the rationale. • Questions provide guidance for action planning and can be used as formative and summative assessment measures of individual or group learning.	• Prioritized research questions are specific, concise, and explicitly linked to the rationale for the study. • Questions provide the structure for data collection and analysis.
Example • How can we improve student writing?	*Example* • How can we improve student writing? • What are our students' writing strengths and weaknesses?	*Example* • How can we improve student writing in grade 4? • What specific strengths and weaknesses are exhibited in our students' nonfiction writing? • What specific lessons or strategies will be most useful in targeting the struggles of our students?	*Example* • How can ongoing assessment help us improve student nonfiction writing in grade 4? • What specific strengths and weaknesses are exhibited in the students' baseline samples, according to our grade-level rubric? • How does the teacher's use of explicit criteria and specific feedback affect quality?

Assessing the Quality of Inquiry Questions

Explanation of Quality Level	Explanation of Quality Level	Explanation of Quality Level
Although this question reveals a focus on student writing, it is not specific enough to guide data collection or analysis.	The addition of the second question provides a bit of guidance for data analysis but still leaves questions about which students and which writing.	Notice that the questions now guide researchers in what type of writing to analyze and from which students. As the questions get more specific, the focus gets more specific and data collection becomes clearer.

Explanation of Quality Level

Here specific strategies are identified, thus pointing to specific data. Notice that the researchers now know what tool they will use for analysis.

Section 3

Personal Learning Journal 3

A personal learning journal allows individual group members to reflect on their own deepening understanding of the work they are engaged in. The questions in this journal prompt provide you with an opportunity to reflect on the work the group has done on inquiry questions.

The journal can be a private thinking tool or, if individuals share after writing, a jumping-off point for group reflection. The journal can be on paper or posted to an online discussion board so that group members can see and respond to one another's thinking.

USING THE TOOL

1. The facilitator of the group meeting (see "Facilitating Collegial Inquiry" on page 122) provides the questions to members of the group and explains that they may respond to all or some of the questions.

   • If you use the journal during a group meeting, provide enough time for thoughtful response.

2. (Optional) Allow for the sharing of individual reflection at the end of a meeting, at the start of a meeting, or between sessions via a discussion board, Google Group, or electronic mailing list.

Personal Learning Journal for Section 3

1. How did the process of generating and refining inquiry questions affect my understanding of the group's work?

2. How has the distinction between exploratory and action-oriented inquiry questions helped me understand the work I am engaged in?

3. Now that I have specific questions, what data am I going to need to collect? Why do I think so?

4. In light of my specific questions, how might I revise my rationale or my criteria for success?

Section 3

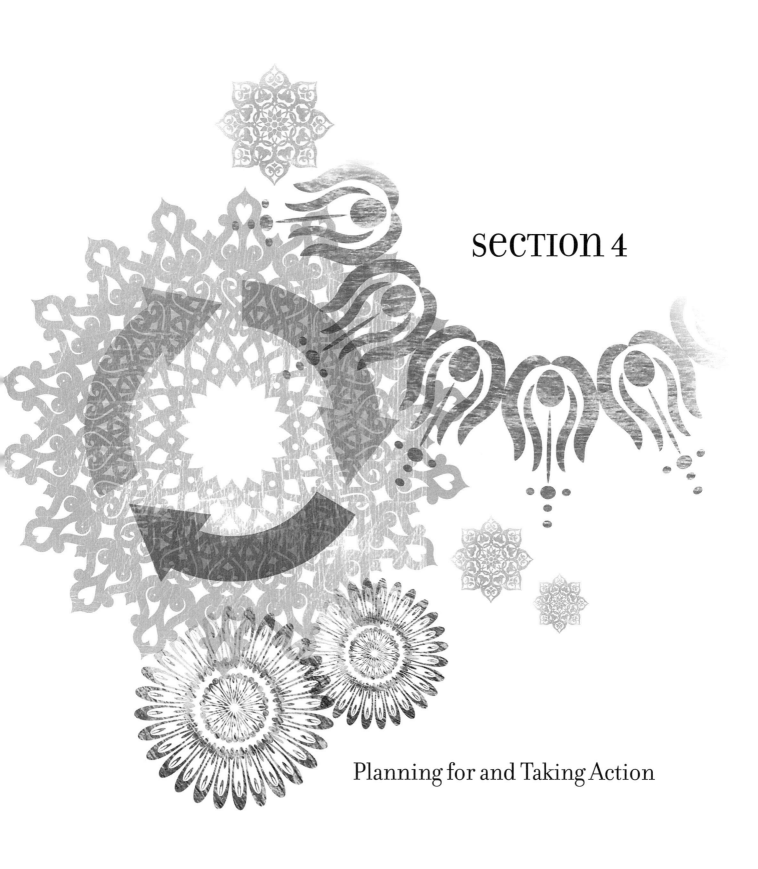

SECTION 4

Planning for and Taking Action

SECTION 4

Planning for and Taking Action

Planning for Action 94

Exploring Possible Actions. 102

Taking Action and Considering Its Effects 104

Personal Learning Journal 4. 107

Section 4

Planning for Action

Having refined the inquiry questions the group would like to pursue (see Section 3 on page 69), you can begin planning action steps. Some common and important actions in the collegial inquiry process are

- using current research and literature
- seeking and using different perspectives on your topic
- using data
- applying new learning
- reflecting regularly
- documenting your journey

The criteria for action planning in the following checklist can help guide your decisions about action steps. Used regularly, it can help you monitor your work and ensure that everyone studies in-depth and takes the time to be thoughtful.

The "Potential Action Items" tool provides specific strategies based on the criteria for rigorous planning that you can use to deepen your study. The strategies can help you decide how to meet or improve a particular area, and they can help you vary your approaches to meet the range of learning styles of those involved in the study.

Based on the potential action items, you can formulate your own action plan—customized to the focus of your study and the nature of your inquiry questions—that meets the defined criteria for high quality.

USING THE TOOL

1. Review the "Criteria for Disciplined and Rigorous Action Planning" to be sure all members of the group understand each measure.

2. As a group, review the list of "Potential Action Items" and discuss which strategies are appealing and applicable to your work.

3. Talk about the advantages and disadvantages of the strategies you are considering.

Planning for Action

4. Create your own action plan modeled after the potential action items, and check that it meets the criteria on the checklist.

5. After several sessions or during each agenda planning session, review the list of criteria to assess the degree to which your work is meeting each criterion.

Criteria for Disciplined and Rigorous Action Planning

☐ The group reads and uses current research and thinking on the topic.

☐ The group accesses and uses multiple perspectives on the topic.

☐ The group members identify and use pertinent new learning in their own practice.

☐ The group members collect and share evidence of applied learning.

☐ The group uses various types of data over the course of the study.

☐ The group uses protocols to guide discussion, data analysis, and sharing.

☐ The group documents its learning and practice over time.

☐ The group regularly reflects on learning, application of learning, and group processes.

Section 4

Planning for Action

Potential Action Items

Criteria (How do we ensure that the inquiry is rigorous?)	Potential Actions (What might we do?)
The group will read and use current research and thinking on the topic.	• Read articles, professional books, dissertations, research papers, research briefs, or conference presentations. • View professional videos or conference presentations. • Attend workshops or conferences.
The group will access and use multiple perspectives on the topic.	• Search for different perspectives by looking to fields outside of education. • Search for different perspectives by looking to other districts, schools, or learning organizations. • Ask questions to gather the perspective of different stakeholders. • Interview colleagues and individuals outside of the work who have different roles, positions, or experiences. • Use surveys or focus groups to gather thinking of others. • Access multiple viewpoints from different thinkers on the same topic or practice.

Section 4

Section 4

Criteria (How do we ensure that the inquiry is rigorous?)	Potential Actions (What might we do?)
The group members will identify and use pertinent new learning in their own practice.	• Individually and collaboratively identify new learning that has occurred and capture it in writing. • Revise existing practices, products, or processes using new learning. • Experiment with new strategies or practices on a small scale. • Individually or collaboratively design and use new lessons, tools, strategies, curriculum, policies, or programs.
The group members will collect and share evidence of applied learning (student work for classroom teachers, teacher work for those working with adults).	• Bring samples (tangible products, videos, audiotapes, photographs) of your own work for peer review. • Bring samples of student work (for teachers) or teacher work (for those working with adult learners) for peer review. • Observe one another and confer about observations. • Examine "before" and "after" samples for change and growth.
The group will use various types of data over the course of the study.	• Collect perceptual data, learning data, and process data related to the study. • Read about and explore various types of data analysis strategies. • Analyze a single piece of data or a data set together to deepen understanding of the data and the process. • Use data to draw conclusions, identify implications, and generate new questions.

Planning for Action

Criteria (How do we ensure that the inquiry is rigorous?)	Potential Actions (What might we do?)
The group will use protocols to guide discussion, data analysis, and sharing.	• Establish criteria for quality discussion, and use them to reflect on discussions. • Experiment with various published protocols for discussion and data analysis.
The group will document its learning and practice over time.	• Maintain agendas over time. • Record or summarize decisions. • Keep individual and group portfolios that capture the work and learning. • Keep copies or bibliographies of the resources you've read and used.
Individuals and the group will regularly reflect on learning, application of learning, and group processes.	• Respond regularly to reflective prompts about learning. • Respond regularly to reflective prompts about group processes. • Set goals to improve working processes. • Review and discuss inquiry questions verbally or in writing. • Regularly revisit and refine questions as necessary. • Keep reflective logs, journals, or blogs about learning, struggles, and new questions.

Source: Used with permission from Giselle O. Martin-Kniep, Learner-Centered Initiatives Ltd., Floral Park, N.Y.

Section 4

Our Action Items

Criteria (How do we ensure that the inquiry is rigorous?)	Actions (What are we going to do?)
The group will read and use current research and thinking on the topic.	
The group will access and use multiple perspectives on the topic.	
The group members will identify and use pertinent new learning in their own practice.	
The group members will collect and share evidence of applied learning (student work for classroom teachers, teacher work for those working with adults).	
The group will use various types of data over the course of the study.	

Section 4

Planning for Action

Criteria (How do we ensure that the inquiry is rigorous?)	Actions (What are we going to do?)
The group will use protocols to guide discussion, data analysis, and sharing.	
The group will document its learning and practice over time.	
Individuals and the group will regularly reflect on learning, application of learning, and group processes.	

Section 4

Exploring Possible Actions

During inquiry, you need to regularly make decisions about the course of action to take to further your inquiry. When several options are appealing or when a group disagrees, it is helpful to think through a rationale for a specific action to clarify your thinking and illuminate the most productive actions. Articulating a rationale forces you to slow down and carefully consider what next steps to take.

USING THE TOOL

1. Choose a facilitator (see "Facilitating Collegial Inquiry" on page 122) to lead the group in brainstorming responses to the question, What are possible next steps or action items for this group?

    - Be sure to brainstorm items that connect to or will support the group in addressing its inquiry questions.
    - Keep the brainstorm to about 2–3 minutes.

2. The facilitator records the group's thinking on chart paper, a whiteboard, or a projector following the three-column chart format illustrated in "Thinking Through Next Steps" on page 103.

3. For each possible action, discuss and articulate a rationale for that action:

    - What would it accomplish?
    - Why would it be worth doing?

    Also, for each action consider the drawbacks, limitations, or unintended consequences.

4. Review the thinking about each action and decide what the group's next steps will be. Be sure to save this chart documenting the groups' thinking; it may prove useful at a future point.

Thinking Through Next Steps

Possible Next Step	Rationale	Limitations, Drawbacks, or Unintended Consequences

Section 4

Taking Action and Considering Its Effects

When it's time to implement new strategies, approaches, or programs, the inquiry group needs to think through how, specifically, it will apply new strategies or approaches. You need to consider what strategies you will undertake, how you will implement them, why you're implementing them, and exactly how you will document the results.

If group members decide to select and apply the same strategy or approach, you can use the tool together to think through implementation as a team. If individuals in a group decide to implement different strategies based on group learning, then you can use this tool independently to plan and document your thinking. Other group members can then review the completed chart, or you can share the information with the group.

If you're using the tool independently, be sure that the documentation accounts for the effect the strategies will have on other learners and other inquiry group members.

USING THE TOOL

1. As a group, select the strategy or approach you will implement, considering what you have learned from the research or professional literature on that strategy.

2. Think about the context for your implementation:

   • When will you use the strategy?

   • Who will you use it with?

   • Under what conditions will you use the strategy?

   • How often will you use it?

   Be sure to make notes about these decisions and keep your plan manageable.

3. Revisit your rationale for selecting the strategy:

   • Why is it suited to your work?

   • What do you hope will happen as a result?

   • How will you and others benefit?

Taking Action and Considering Its Effects

4. Because every setting is different, think about whether you might need to modify or adjust the strategy in any way. These modifications should make sense given who you are, who you work with, and your work conditions.

5. Write down the specific methods you will use to document your implementation and capture the results. It is crucial that you keep track of your implementation. The results may include

- The effect the strategy has on other learners.
- The influence using the strategy has had on your thinking or practice.

Taking Action and Considering Its Effects

Thinking Through Implementation

Goal (strategy or approach we will embed in our practice):

Context	Rationale	Modifications	Documentation

Personal Learning Journal 4

A personal learning journal allows individual group members to reflect on their own deepening understanding of the work they are engaged in. The questions in this journal prompt provide you with an opportunity to reflect on the decisions the group has made about the actions you will take together.

The journal can be a private thinking tool or, if individuals share after writing, a jumping-off point for group reflection. The journal can be on paper or posted to an online discussion board so that group members can see and respond to one another's thinking.

USING THE TOOL

1. The facilitator of the group meeting (see "Facilitating Collegial Inquiry" on page 122) provides the questions to members of the group and explains that they may respond to all or some of the questions.

   • If you use the journal during a group meeting, provide enough time for thoughtful response.

2. (Optional) Allow for the sharing of individual reflection at the end of a meeting, at the start of a meeting, or between sessions via a discussion board, Google Group, or electronic mailing list.

Section 4

Personal Learning Journal for Section 4

1. How well is my group planning for the work we do together?

2. How does my group make decisions about what to do next? Do we consider the decisions carefully?

3. What might my group do to improve its planning?

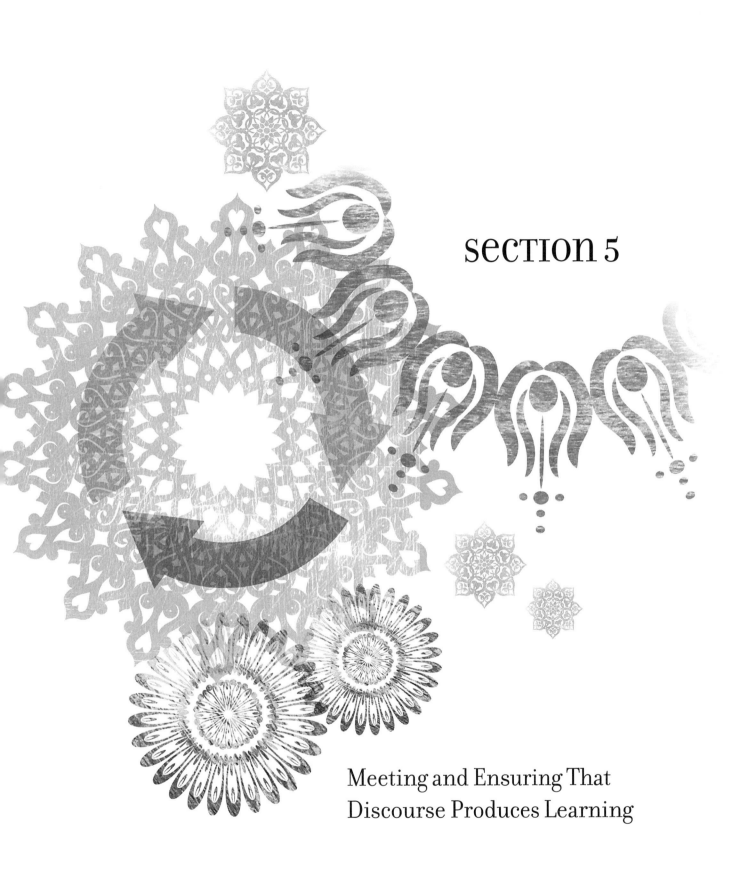

SECTION 5

Meeting and Ensuring That
Discourse Produces Learning

Meeting and Ensuring That Discourse Produces Learning

Planning an Inquiry Meeting 112

Creating an Agenda. 114

Establishing Ground Rules 120

Facilitating Collegial Inquiry 122

Keeping an Eye on Discourse 128

Assessing the Quality of Text-Based Discussion. 132

Evaluating Your Contribution to Discussion. 134

Personal Learning Journal 5. 136

Section 5

Planning an Inquiry Meeting

In planning for your next meeting or series of meetings, it's important that the group's plan of action—what it decides to *do*—aligns with the inquiry questions that you have chosen to focus on. If you cannot draw explicit connections between your actions and the inquiry question, you should reconsider your action.

This tool, which is particularly helpful for those who may not have much experience shaping their own agendas for meetings, provides a simple way to think through the planning of a meeting in terms of logistics and content.

USING THE TOOL

1. Determine when and where the next meeting will take place, as well as who will facilitate it (see also "Facilitating Collegial Inquiry" on page 122).

2. Think about the content and question focus for the forthcoming meeting or meetings.

3. Identify the reason for including each agenda item.

4. Discuss what materials the group will need and what each group member will need to do in preparation for the meeting.

Section 5

Guiding Questions for Meeting Planning

LOGISTICAL BASICS

☐ What is the date and time of the next meeting?

☐ How long will the meeting be?

☐ Where will the group meet?

☐ Who will facilitate the meeting?

CONTENT

☐ Which inquiry question (if the group has several) will the meeting focus on?

☐ What will the group do together? Or what will the agenda items be?

☐ Why is each item in the agenda? How does it support the inquiry and relate to the question?

Agenda Item	Rationale/Connection to the Inquiry Question

PREPARATION

☐ What materials will the group need to gather or create before the meeting?

☐ What will individuals need to do to get ready for the group meeting?

Creating an Agenda

Careful planning will contribute to the success of an inquiry group, and agenda planning includes working with the questions you've chosen as the focus of your inquiry, identifying appropriate actions and resources, and deciding how to document your work.

This tool is designed to be completed by the meeting's facilitator (see "Facilitating Collegial Inquiry" on page 122). Whether the group has a single meeting facilitator or rotates the responsibilities, the template provides a consistent form for the agenda and embeds an opportunity to reflect on the group's work using the criteria for rigorous inquiry. It is also a documentation strategy in itself, because it can preserve the history of a group's inquiry over time.

USING THE TOOL

1. Review the decisions the group made at the last meeting, and fill in what the group agreed to do in preparation for this meeting.

2. Insert the inquiry question or questions that the planned agenda is focusing on. If there seems to be a misalignment between the questions and the previous agenda items, note it for the group to discuss.

3. Identify the artifacts or methods with which the group will be documenting its work.

4. Identify the agenda items and approximate times for each item, taking into consideration the total time the group has together.

5. Decide whether there will be an individual or group reflection, the focus of the reflection, and the method of the reflection (e.g., whole-group or small-group discussion, written notes). (See Section 7 on page 175 for more information about reflection.)

Agenda Template

Date: _____

At our last meeting, we agreed to do the following prior to this meeting:

-

-

TODAY'S INQUIRY QUESTION FOCUS

_____

_____

AGENDA ITEMS

-

-

-

- Planning for the next session

- Reflection (individual or group)

DOCUMENTATION STRATEGIES

_____

_____

_____

_____

_____

Section 5

PLANNING FOR THE NEXT SESSION

Individual action items that need to be done before *the next meeting:*

-

-

Question for the next meeting:

Action items to be completed at *the next meeting:*

-

-

-

Resources or materials needed:

-

-

-

REFLECTION

Which criteria for rigorous inquiry are we meeting (✓) and which do we need to tend to?

☐ Using current research and thinking on our topic.

☐ Accessing and using multiple perspectives on the topic.

☐ Using pertinent new learning in our practice.

☐ Collecting and sharing evidence of applied learning.

☐ Using various types of data.

☐ Using protocols to guide discussion, data analysis, and sharing.

☐ Documenting our learning and practice.

☐ Reflecting on learning, application of learning, and group processes.

Section 5

Example Agenda

Date: February 4, 2010

At our last meeting, we agreed to do the following prior to this meeting:

- Break into three triads. Each triad chooses a reading about learning styles from three different experts.
- Duplicate the reading for the whole group, read it, and prepare to teach the important points to the other groups at this meeting.

TODAY'S INQUIRY QUESTION FOCUS

1. What are the various learning styles and multiple intelligences?
2. Do we know our own learning styles and intelligences?

AGENDA ITEMS

- Teach one another about learning styles and multiple intelligences from different articles. (30)
- Take a learning styles inventory. (15)
- Discussion: What did each of us learn about our learning styles? How are our learning styles reflected in our teaching styles? (15)
- Choose an inventory to use with our students. (5)
- Plan for the next session. (10)
- Reflection (written): How is my learning about learning styles changing the way I think about my instruction? (5)

DOCUMENTATION STRATEGIES

- 3 articles/chapters in our binder
- facilitator notes from discussion
- completed inventories
- written reflections

Section 5

PLANNING FOR THE NEXT SESSION

Individual action items that need to be done before *the next meeting:*

- Each member will identify three different students from his or her class, use the inventory with each student, and collect various work samples from each student.

Question for the next meeting:

- How can we identify the learning styles of a child?

Action items to be completed at *the next meeting:*

- Each member will select one student and present a case study to other members using the inventory and work samples.
- The group will discuss each child and brainstorm strategies to match the learning styles or intelligences of that child.

Resources or materials needed:

- copies of various inventories
- protocol for case study discussion (facilitator will locate this)

REFLECTION

Which criteria for rigorous inquiry are we meeting (✓) and which do we need to tend to?

- ☑ Using current research and thinking on our topic.

- ☑ Accessing and using multiple perspectives on the topic.

- ☐ Using pertinent new learning in our practice. (*We are getting ready to do this.*)

- ☐ Collecting and sharing evidence of applied learning. (*We are getting ready to do this.*)

- ☐ Using various types of data.

- ☐ Using protocols to guide discussion, data analysis, and sharing. (*We will use one next time.*)

- ☐ Documenting our learning and practice.

- ☑ Reflecting on learning, application of learning, and group processes.

Section 5

ASCD 119

Establishing Ground Rules

Ground rules, when established by a group, can serve as a contract of sorts that guides the group while you work, helping you achieve your goals. Generally, ground rules help a group make explicit the assumptions and beliefs that individual members have about how to work together.

You may choose to develop ground rules together at the start of the group's inquiry or when they seem to be needed. When establishing ground rules, it is helpful to be as specific as possible, phrase the rules so that they describe behaviors, and use simple language. The following guidelines can be helpful:

- Keep the ground rules focused on specific behaviors in the form of dos and don'ts.
- Use simple, active language.
- Share the rules with the group and with visitors regularly.

You can include the rules on agendas, post them where everyone can see them, share them with visitors, and revisit them if the group struggles to work well together or if issues arise that impede the group's progress.

USING THE TOOL

1. As a group, review the guidelines above and refer to the example if needed.
2. For about 2–3 minutes, brainstorm ground rules of your own as a group.
3. Review each rule to be sure that everyone agrees with it. Discuss, revise, or eliminate rules that you cannot agree on.
4. Prioritize the rules so that the most important are at the top of the list.

Section 5

Example Ground Rules

- We will start and end on time.

- We will come prepared.

- We will follow through on action items that we commit to.

- We will stay on task and avoid side conversations.

- We will make phone calls and take care of other business on breaks.

- We will listen respectfully to one another.

- We will listen to increase understanding, rather than think about what we want to say next.

Section 5

Facilitating Collegial Inquiry

Whether you have a designated facilitator for the inquiry group or you rotate the responsibilities among group members, the facilitator should understand the inquiry process and all of its complexities. In addition, the meeting's leader must know how to manage and orchestrate the work of a group of individuals.

The rubrics in this tool describe facilitation at different levels and provide an image of what high-quality facilitation looks like. They also offer various reflection points for facilitators and the groups they work with. As a group, you can use the rubrics to clarify the role of or provide feedback to a facilitator. As an individual facilitator, you can use the rubrics for self-assessment and goal setting.

USING THE TOOL

For Individual Self-Assessment

1. Read across the first rubric and circle where you think you fall for each criterion.

    - If you believe you exhibit the criterion listed, you should be able to identify a moment or example from your practice that supports your assessment.

    - If you struggle to identify a specific example of where you exhibited that criterion, then you may need to move your assessment down one level.

2. Use the space below the rubric to write

    - Your examples.

    - Your thinking about your practice.

    - Any questions you may have.

    - Specific goals that you can set to improve your practice.

Facilitating Collegial Inquiry

3. Follow the same process for the next two rubrics.

For Group Clarification of the Facilitation Role

1. Allow time for the group to read through the rubrics.

2. Discuss the following questions about the role of a facilitator:

   • Which characteristics embedded in the rubrics do you think are the most important? Why?

   • How would you characterize the role of the facilitator? Can you think of a metaphor that would help us understand the role?

   • What specific skills and abilities related to facilitation do you think are most critical for our group? Why?

   • Was there anything about the criteria in these rubrics that surprised you? Why?

Rubrics for Quality Facilitation

PERSONAL ATTRIBUTES OF FACILITATOR

Unsatisfactory	Developing	Proficient	Exemplary		
Doesn't believe in the process of learning through collegial inquiry.	Expresses some doubts about the process of learning through collegial inquiry.	Can articulate the value of the process of learning through collegial inquiry.	Shows enthusiasm about the process of learning through collegial inquiry.		
Is disorganized and rigid.	Shows unevenness in organizational skills and is rarely flexible.	Is organized and flexible when the group requests changes.	Is organized and structured, but flexible and adaptable when necessary.		
Is too focused on the agenda or too inexperienced to respond to group dynamics.	Has minimal understanding of group dynamics.	Is aware of group dynamics.	Shows deep understanding of the dynamics of the group.		
Is critical of others' opinions and ideas.	Accepts opinions that are similar to his or her own.	Accepts diverse opinions.	Accepts diverse opinions and helps the group use them effectively.		
Is unsure of himself or herself.	Shows some unease.	Is confident.	Is at ease, self-assured, and confident.		

My Thinking and Questions

My Goals for Improvement

FACILITATOR'S PREPARATION

Unsatisfactory	Developing	Proficient	Exemplary
Has no agenda or has a hidden agenda.	Forms the agenda without input or feedback from the group.	Organizes the agenda in response to group needs, and shares it with the group for feedback.	Guides the group in creating the agenda in preparation for the next meeting.
Doesn't establish ground rules or a time frame to guide group work.	Develops arbitrary ground rules and time frames for the group.	Develops helpful ground rules and time frames, then revises them with assistance from the group.	Guides the group in developing helpful ground rules and time frames.
Assumes others will take responsibility for planning details and gathering resources and materials; does not follow through to be sure everything is completed prior to the meeting and fails to create a contingency plan.	Takes some responsibility for planning details and gathering resources and materials for group meetings; doesn't complete all tasks prior to the meeting and fails to create a contingency plan.	Takes full responsibility for planning details and gathering resources and materials for group meetings; completes everything prior to the meeting.	Shares responsibility for planning details and gathering resources and materials for group meetings; ensures that everything is complete prior to meetings.

My Thinking and Questions

My Goals for Improvement

Section 5

MANAGEMENT OF THE FACILITATION PROCESS

Unsatisfactory	Developing	Proficient	Exemplary
Sets a tone that makes all uncomfortable or defensive, and discourages risk taking of any sort.	Sets a business-like tone that may be uncomfortable for some.	Sets a tone that allows participants to feel comfortable.	Sets a tone that allows participants to feel comfortable and free to take intellectual risks.
Allows the group to work without reference to an agenda, and fails to help the group stay on task.	Reviews the agenda at the start but frequently allows the group to stray from the task at hand.	Clarifies the agenda and assures that the group stays on task.	Clarifies the agenda, ensures that the group stays on task, and strategically adjusts course when necessary.
Repeatedly allows certain members to monopolize the conversation and others to not participate at all, thereby frustrating the group.	Works to try to get all members to participate but occasionally allows someone to monopolize the conversation or decision making.	Assures balanced participation by all group members.	Mediates conversation, asks clarifying and extending questions, and achieves balanced participation by all group members.
Fails to wait for participants to think, and rarely summarizes group discussions or decisions.	Sometimes uses wait time; summarizes at the end of meetings only.	Uses wait time consistently; summarizes group discussion or decisions during the process as needed.	Uses wait time strategically; summarizes group discussion or decisions during the process as needed.
Often ignores or dismisses participant comments.	Needs to validate participant comments more often.	Validates all participant comments.	Uses knowledge about group dynamics to validate or challenge participant comments.

Facilitating Collegial Inquiry

Unsatisfactory	Developing	Proficient	Exemplary
Operates with disregard for ground rules or without them at all.	Overemphasizes ground rules, causing discomfort for group members.	Enforces ground rules consistently when necessary.	Reminds group of ground rules and guides group members in enforcing them.
Fails to assign roles.	Assigns roles to group members arbitrarily, without regard for personal strength.	Assigns roles to group members, matching roles to strengths.	Facilitates role assignment when needed, helping the group match roles to members' strengths.

My Thinking and Questions

My Goals for Improvement

Keeping an Eye on Discourse

To enhance learning, the conversation of an inquiry group should be balanced, thoughtful, and respectful—whether you're talking about a text, selected data, a strategy, or a decision. Observing and creating a visual map of discourse can help a group see how it operates during discussion.

By examining the illustration of discourse, you become more aware of the group's dynamics and can make adjustments to improve the quality of conversation. The tool is particularly helpful when a group is struggling to have conversations that feel productive and produce new learning, when one or more members dominate conversation, or when some members are particularly quiet and seemingly disengaged in conversation.

USING THE TOOL

For the Group

1. Identify a process observer to monitor the group's discussion. This may be the facilitator (see "Facilitating Collegial Inquiry" on page 122) or another volunteer from the group.

2. Have a discussion, which the observer will watch. (See process observer steps below.)

3. After the observer has shared notes, respond to one or more of the reflection questions about the balance and patterns related to your discourse.

For the Process Observer

1. Create a visual representation of how group members are seated, using initials or first names to indicate individuals.

2. Watch the conversation for 10–15 minutes, and tally who speaks by placing check marks next to individual's initial or name in the chart.

3. Use arrows to indicate who speaks in response to someone else and show the pattern of conversation in the group.

4. After the discussion, share your observations and graphic with the group.

Keeping an Eye on Discourse

Mapping Discourse

Use the space below to create a visual representation that shows how group members are seated. Tally who speaks and use arrows to indicate the flow or pattern of conversation and responses.

Facilitator or Group Reflection Questions

1. How balanced is the conversation the group is having? Are all members contributing? Is anyone dominating in ways that are counterproductive? Are there members who need to be encouraged to participate?

2. If there is an imbalance, what might be the reasons for it?

3. Does the group need to continue to pay attention to patterns of conversation?

Example of Mapping Discourse

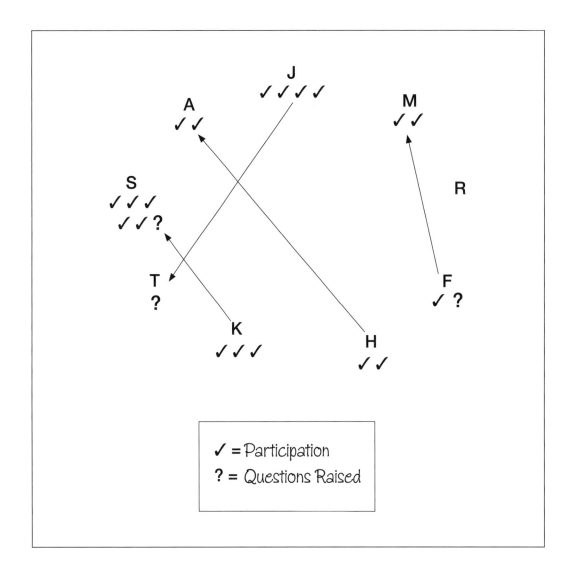

Facilitator or Group Reflection Questions

1. How balanced is the conversation the group is having? Are all members contributing? Is anyone dominating in ways that are counterproductive? Are there members who need to be encouraged to participate?

   Almost all members participated in the conversation over the last 15 minutes, but two members engaged in dialogue for a good chunk of time. We also had two very quiet members.

2. If there is an imbalance, what might be the reasons for it?

   The two members who spoke for the longest time seemed to have more experience with the strategy we were discussing.

3. Does the group need to continue to pay attention to patterns of conversation?

   We might want to encourage the participation of the quiet members by inviting them into the conversation or directing questions toward them.

Section 5

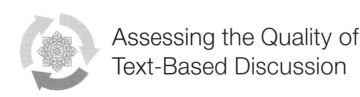

Assessing the Quality of Text-Based Discussion

The quality of discourse is an important factor in the success of collegial inquiry, and this is especially true when outside reading is involved. The purposes for bringing a text to a group's inquiry are to deepen understanding and broaden perspective. This tool provides criteria for high-quality, text-based discussion that can help you enhance a process that many assume they are already good at.

By identifying and discussing the characteristics of high-quality discourse, individuals and the entire group will be able to have conversations that produce learning. You can then use the discourse criteria to reflect on what you do well and ways you can improve. The tool is particularly helpful when a group is struggling to have conversations that feel productive and produce new learning.

USING THE TOOL

1. Before discussing the text, review the criteria for a high-quality, text-based discussion. As a group, clarify any criteria you have questions about.
2. Identify a process observer to monitor the group's use of the criteria. This may be the facilitator (see "Facilitating Collegial Inquiry" on page 122) or another volunteer from the group.

For the Process Observer

3. Listen and analyze the conversation.
4. As the group has the discussion, place check marks or tallies next to the criteria that you see and hear.
5. Make additional notes about talking points, segments of the text members reread and referenced, and questions during discussion.
6. After 10–15 minutes, stop the group and report back about what you have observed and heard.
7. Ask the group about what they may want to work on for the remainder of the discussion.

Assessing the Quality of Text-Based Discussion

Checklist for High-Quality, Text-Based Discussion

Text discussed: Date:_____

Observed	Characteristics of High-Quality Discussion
	Conversation stays focused on topics relevant to the text.
	Members listen attentively and build on one another's ideas.
	Members reference the text specifically by page number and location and find places in the text to discuss or support their ideas.
	Members agree or disagree respectfully.
	Members draw on their own experiences.
	Members refocus when necessary.
	Members ask questions of one another.
	Members paraphrase what others say.
	Members help everyone participate so that even the quieter or more passive members speak.

Talking Points	Questions Raised

Section 5

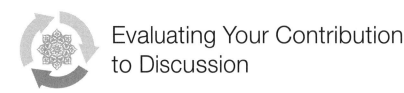

Evaluating Your Contribution to Discussion

Along with a group reflecting together on the quality of its discourse, it is also valuable for individual members to examine how they are contributing to a group's inquiry during discussion. With this tool, you can review the actions that can enhance discourse and privately consider your participation and set goals for improvement.

USING THE TOOL

1. Set aside 10–15 minutes of a group meeting to allow individuals to self-assess and set goals.

2. Individually, review the criteria and reflect on recent discussions you have participated in. Decide if this is an action that you rarely, inconsistently, or consistently practice during discussion.

3. Select one action that you believe you can improve on, and set a goal for a coming discussion or meeting. Make the goals as specific as possible.

4. (Optional) Share your goal with another colleague or the entire group. Ask your colleague or the group to help you reach it or give you feedback after the next discussion.

Section 5

Self-Assessment for Individual Contribution to Discussion

Key: 1 = I rarely practice this.
2 = I am inconsistent in my practice.
3 = I am consistent in my practice.

Criteria	How consistently do I practice this?	What specific goal can I set for our next discussion?
I strive to contribute to each discussion in significant and meaningful ways.		
When we use a text or a data set, I explicitly go back to the text to draw from it and connect my ideas to it.		
I raise questions for my group that will push our thinking and deepen our understanding.		
I paraphrase what others say in an effort to sharpen my listening skills and communicate that I am listening carefully.		
I make explicit connections to the ideas of other group members in an effort to understand their perspectives and build on them or provide an alternative perspective.		
I am conscious of not talking too much, because I know that my group members also have significant contributions to make.		
I make explicit efforts to invite colleagues into discussion if I notice that one or several are quiet.		

Section 5

Personal Learning Journal 5

A personal learning journal allows individual group members to reflect on their own deepening understanding of the work they are engaged in. The questions in this journal prompt provide you with an opportunity to reflect on the quality of discussion the group is having and the facilitation of the group.

The journal can be a private thinking tool or, if individuals share after writing, a jumping-off point for group reflection. The journal can be on paper or posted to an online discussion board so that group members can see and respond to one another's thinking.

USING THE TOOL

1. The facilitator of the group meeting (see "Facilitating Collegial Inquiry" on page 122) provides the questions to members of the group and explains that they may respond to all or some of the questions.

   - If you use the journal during a group meeting, provide enough time for thoughtful response.

2. (Optional) Allow for the sharing of individual reflection at the end of a meeting, at the start of a meeting, or between sessions via a discussion board, Google Group, or electronic mailing list.

Personal Learning Journal for Section 5

FACILITATION OF THE GROUP

1. How well is our group using ground rules? What do we need to work on?

2. What are the strengths of the facilitator(s) who have been managing the work of our team?

3. What do I believe the group needs to do to support the facilitator(s)?

QUALITY OF DISCUSSION

1. How are the group discussions contributing to the learning of the group? How are they contributing to my own learning?

2. What are the strengths of my group when it comes to discussion?

3. What do I think the group needs to work on to improve the quality of its discourse?

4. What personal goals have I set for contributing to discussions? Why have I set these goals?

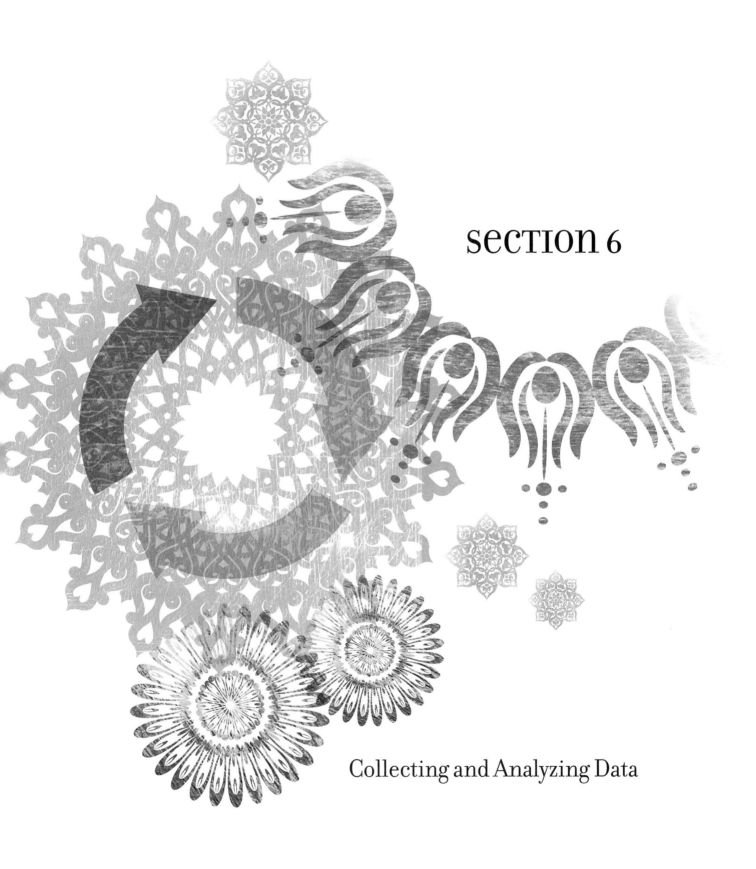

SECTION 6

Collecting and Analyzing Data

Collecting and Analyzing Data

Identifying Data Sources for Collegial Inquiry 142

Matching Data Sources with Inquiry Questions 146

Planning Data Collection 148

Assessing the Quality of Data Collection. 152

Organizing Data for Analysis. 154

Analyzing Data by Identifying Themes 158

Drawing Conclusions from Data. 166

Capturing the Group's Learning from Data Analysis. 170

Personal Learning Journal 6. 172

Section 6

Identifying Data Sources for Collegial Inquiry

During the inquiry cycle, data can help an inquiry group define its work, monitor its implementation and learning, and adjust or refine the collegial inquiry process. In all three cases, you can use various types of data, including those beyond test scores or quantifiable information—which educators all too often think of as the only types of data.

This tool can help you see the many types of data available in schools that can support inquiry related to leading, teaching, and learning. When you need to make decisions about data that will inform your work or that will capture the results of your actions, this tool can provide a menu of data sources. You can revisit it over time and use alternative sources of data collection that can support deep understanding.

USING THE TOOL

1. As a group, think about the purpose for the data you will collect.

    • Are data needed to investigate the current state of practice?

    • Are data needed to capture the results of actions taken?

2. Review the possible data sources one at a time, and make notes in response to the questions.

3. Identify at least three data sources that seem realistic and manageable and that you have designated as being able to provide the information you need.

Possible Data Sources for Collegial Inquiry

Data Source	Will it provide the information we need?	Is it possible to collect without disrupting teaching or learning?	Will it be manageable?
Anecdotal Records Written descriptions of events, often about what a person says or does in a specific situation. Notes may include a description of events that precede and follow the specific event.			
Documents Tangible data sources that may represent student or adult learning, school processes or performance, or district processes or performance. Examples include samples of student work, teacher lessons, curriculum maps, letters, memos, policies, and teacher– or school-made tests.			
Learning Journals Personal accounts of learning usually kept on a regular basis. They may contain questions, insights, new thinking, feelings, or reactions. These capture the changing thinking of individuals and can be an important data source for a group.			

Identifying Data Sources for Collegial Inquiry

Data Source	Will it provide the information we need?	Is it possible to collect without disrupting teaching or learning?	Will it be manageable?
Logs A record of the number and durations of specific actions or events over time, typically organized with respect to time. Examples include a log of referrals to the principal or a log of who asks questions in a classroom during a week of lessons.			
Observation Notes A record of a person's observations during an event or series of events.			
Portfolios Purposeful collections of materials that include the keeper's reflections on the artifacts included.			
Questionnaires Written questions requiring written responses. Questions can be open-ended (asking for information in the respondent's own words) or closed (asking the respondent to choose a response from a list).			
Interviews One-on-one conversations that can be recorded through note taking or tape.			
Audio Recordings Tape or digital audio records of conferences, meetings, discussions, or lessons.			

Section 6

Identifying Data Sources for Collegial Inquiry

Data Source	Will it provide the information we need?	Is it possible to collect without disrupting teaching or learning?	Will it be manageable?
Video Recordings Can capture many types of events, such as lessons, group performances, or processes, and allow for careful analysis later.			
Photographs and Slides Can capture work that is too large to hold and share easily. Can be analyzed later and described carefully.			

Source: Summarized from *The Action Research Planner* (3rd ed.), by S. Kemmis and R. McTaggart (Eds.), 1988, Waurn Ponds, Australia: Deakin University Press.

Matching Data Sources with Inquiry Questions

To help ensure that the group gathers the information it needs to promote learning, sources of data need to match the inquiry questions the group is pursuing. In addition, you should gather data for each inquiry question from several sources to make certain your conclusions are supported by multiple measures.

When you are planning or framing your inquiry, this tool will allow you to think about the fit among each source of data, the information it will provide, and your inquiry questions. Once you have identified the research questions that are most important to the group (see Section 3 on page 69), you can set out a plan for data collection using this tool.

USING THE TOOL

1. As a group, think about data sources that will provide information to help answer each research question. Consider both data sources that are already available and those you may need to incorporate into your practice.

2. List all possible data sources, and then select at least three that will provide useful information.

Section 6

Matching Data Sources with Inquiry Questions

Inquiry Question	Data Collection Strategies (What data will help us answer the question? Or, how might we capture the answer to this question?)
Example Which reading comprehension strategies are my students using well?	*Example* Source 1: conference notes Source 2: reflective journal entries Source 3: think-aloud transcripts
	Source 1: Source 2: Source 3:
	Source 1: Source 2: Source 3:

Planning Data Collection

Collecting various types of data allows a group to consider its work through different lenses and, at any point in the inquiry process, supports the development of more refined inquiry questions and action.

The categorization Victoria Bernhardt defines in *Data Analysis for Comprehensive Schoolwide Improvement* divides data into four groups: perceptual data, student learning data, school process data, and demographic data.[1] Collecting data from each of the groups can help provide balance and a more accurate snapshot of the issue at hand. This tool can help you find different types data sources to address an inquiry question.

USING THE TOOL

1. As a group, review the definition of each type of data.
2. Identify possible data sources that fit each type and that could provide relevant information for the inquiry question you are working with. Think about

   • What data may be relevant to our inquiry?

   • What data sources already exist?

   • How might we capture the perceptual data that we need?

---

[1] Bernhardt, V. L. (1998). *Data analysis for comprehensive schoolwide improvement.* Larchmont, NY: Eye on Education.

Planning Data Collection by Type

Inquiry Question: _____

_____

Type	Definition*	Data Source
Perceptual Data	• Data that capture what people think or perceive and include their values, beliefs, attitudes, and observations. • Often captured in interviews, question-naires, and through observation.	
Student Learning Data	• Any data source that captures student learning. • Sources may include quiz or test scores, standardized test scores, student work samples, performances, portfolios, or presentations.	
School Process Data	• Data that define what schools and teachers are doing to get learning results. • Sources may include instructional strategies, programs, resources, curriculum, and classroom practices.	

Planning Data Collection

Type	Definition*	Data Source
Demographic Data	• Data that describe the makeup of a class, school, or district. • Includes information such as enrollment, ethnicities, socioeconomic status, and language proficiency levels.	

*Source: From *Data Analysis for Comprehensive Schoolwide Improvement* (p. 15), by V. L. Bernhardt, 1998, Larchmont, NY: Eye on Education.

Example of Planning Data Collection by Type

Inquiry Question: Which reading comprehension strategies are my students using well?

Type	Data Source
Perceptual Data	• Teachers' observations of which strategies students are using well. • Students' thinking about which strategies they are using well.
Student Learning Data	• Student responses to comprehension questions targeted to specific strategies. • Student reading response journal entries. • Students' recorded think-alouds.
School Process Data	• Teacher lesson plans that focus on reading comprehension. • Instructional materials designed to support reading comprehension. • Curriculum maps across grade levels that detail reading comprehension instructional efforts.
Demographic Data	• The class makeup in terms of native English speakers and English language learners.

Assessing the Quality of Data Collection

To help ensure that the group is paying attention to the key principles of using data well, such as using multiple data sources of different types and keeping the data collection manageable, you should assess the quality of your data collection over time.

The rubric in this tool can help you decide where you fall on the continuum of quality. Based on the result, you can consider revising your data collection strategies if necessary.

USING THE TOOL

1. As a group, read the criteria for low-level to high-level data collection. Assess whether your data collection plan meets all of the criteria for each lower level before moving to the next.

2. If the group identifies a specific criterion that it does not meet, go back and revise your data collection plan.

Rubric for Data Collection

Undeveloped	Emerging	Developed	Exemplary
• The inquiry group has yet to determine what specific techniques it will use for gathering data.	• The inquiry group has generally identified data it will collect. • The inquiry group hasn't identified — What specific kind of data. — How much data. — When it will gather the data. — For what purpose it is collecting the data.	• The inquiry group has a specific data collection plan, but it may be unmanageable given the group's available time. • The plan includes multiple sources of data with specifics about type, amounts, and timing of data collection. • Data collection will capture actions taken and results of actions taken.	• The inquiry group has a specific, realistic, and manageable data collection plan. • The plan includes multiple sources of data of varying types with specifics about amounts and timing of data collection. • Data collection will capture actions taken, results of actions (if proactive inquiry), and the group members' changing thinking.

Organizing Data for Analysis

Once you're well into the inquiry process, the group has often gathered several sets of data that you need to analyze. The first step in getting ready to analyze data is to organize them by type and decide how to go about your analysis.

This tool allows a team to look at the big picture of the data at hand, think about how to analyze them, and even plan for sharing the work of analysis.

USING THE TOOL

1. Gather all the different sets of data (e.g., observations, student products, interview transcripts, photographs, test scores, student and teacher reflections) and bring them to a group meeting. You could also have the facilitator collect and organize data from group members prior to the meeting.

2. List each set of data in the first column, and label it by type (see "Planning Data Collection" on page 148) in the second column.

3. Think about what you want to know from this set of data. Then, to help you stay focused if data answer more than one question, write what you want to know in the form of a question in the third column. This question may be your main inquiry question or may be a smaller question that supports it.

4. Think about a strategy for analyzing each set of data, and describe it in the last column. For example, you could consider the following:

   • Are tallies enough?

   • Do we have criteria in a checklist or rubric?

   • Are we looking for patterns? (If so, see "Analyzing Data by Identifying Themes" on page 158 and "Drawing Conclusions from Data" on page 166.)

5. As a group, discuss the analysis strategies you brainstormed and determine the ones you will undertake.

Organizing Data for Analysis

What data do we have?	What type of data are they? (perceptual data, student learning data, school process data, demographic data)	What do we want to know from the data?	How should we analyze this data set?

Examples of Organizing Data for Analysis

Example Inquiry Group	What data do we have?	What type of data are they?	What do we want to know from the data?	How should we analyze this data set?
Group 1: Student Questioning Ability	Student-generated questions on index cards	Student learning data	What kinds of questions are students able to ask in the context of social studies?	Sort the questions into two categories: • convergent—quick and easy, text explicit • divergent—open-ended, more than one right answer, need more time to answer
Group 2: Reading Comprehension	Reading conference notes	Perceptual data, student and teacher	• Which reading comprehension strategies can students name? • Which reading comprehension strategies do students say they are using when they read?	• Highlight explicit naming of strategies inside conference notes. • Underline descriptions of strategies that may not be explicitly named. • Tally strategies for the entire class.

Section 6

Example Inquiry Group	What data do we have?	What type of data are they?	What do we want to know from the data?	How should we analyze this data set?
Group 3: Teacher Lesson Planning	Individual lesson plans with revisions	School process data	• What are teachers' specific strengths in designing lessons? • What areas of lesson design do teachers struggle with? • What are the next steps in terms of supporting teachers in lesson design?	• Assess each lesson using the school checklist. • Tally the areas of the checklist targeted for revision. • Assess the success of revisions. • Identify the groups' strengths and struggles related to the criteria on the checklist.

Analyzing Data by Identifying Themes

Often, collegial inquiry includes the use of nonnumerical data. To begin to analyze the data, you need to identify patterns that describe the data succinctly. By reducing data to themes, you can more easily describe them, discuss them, and use them to answer inquiry questions or generate new questions or actions.

You can modify the basic procedure of coding data and identifying themes, which this tool describes, to fit many types of data. How you use the process depends on the question you want to answer. Next, you can use "Drawing Conclusions from Data" on page 166 to consider implications or new questions from your analysis.

USING THE TOOL

1. As individuals or working in pairs or triads, read through the entire data set without making any marks. On the first read-through, your goal is to get a sense of the whole and look for connections to the question you want to answer.

2. Read through the data again, this time underlining key phrases that are significant and related to the question you are trying to answer.

3. As you read and underline key phrases, notice the themes that seem to be emerging and write them down in the margin or on a separate piece of paper. For example, if you notice that several phrases are related to "use of time," you would jot a note with that possible theme.

4. Identify codes for themes. For example, you may code "use of time" with a "T" or another symbol. Your codes may be whatever you want, but be sure to keep a key for reference.

5. Read the phrases again, this time applying your codes to the underlined phrases in the data.

   • You can apply more than one code to a segment of data.

   • You may have segments that do not fit your codes. When this happens, you will need to create a new code for that segment.

6. Summarize your analysis by describing the data.

    • Count the number of times each code was used and then create summarizing state-ments. For example, "Six students mentioned that they struggle in peer review" or "The questions asked most often was, How do we find time to revise our curriculum?"

    • It is also helpful to make summarizing statements about items that are mentioned infrequently. For example, "Only 2 of the 34 students spoke about the final presenta-tion as helpful to their learning."

7. Use "Drawing Conclusions from Data" on page 166 to think about implications or new questions.

Data Coding Template

Question: _____

Data source: _____

THEME KEY

Theme	Code

Data:	Theme Codes

Analyzing Data by Identifying Themes

Theme	Summary Statement

Example 1 of Coding Data

Question: How are teachers adjusting their practice and applying their new learning about assessment?

Data source: Teachers' responses to a reflection prompt

THEME KEY

Theme	Code
Changing thinking about assessment	A
Focusing on the feedback process	F
Using classroom assessment tools, such as rubrics, checklists, and conference notes	CT
Sharing with colleagues	SC

Data: Teacher Responses	Theme Codes
1. I assess the lessons of teachers whom I observe.	A
2. During conversations with teachers, especially difficult ones, I've learned to ask questions in the feedback process, whether online or in one-to-one meetings.	F
3. I created additional tools to document the writing/project process. These included a conference sheet, a summative assessment with a reflection checklist for students, a revised storyboard, and a revised final project rubric. I have also spoken to colleagues in reference to our work. I presented the moments of assessment piece at a PD for the entire school.	CT SC
4. I am definitely thinking about assessments more and what constitutes an assessment. Now, I am using and creating my own rubrics as well as checklists for things like group discussion and participation to help keep focus.	A CT
5. I pay attention to the feedback from formal assessments more. I'm making the language of my rubrics more student-friendly. I use rubrics more during the process and try to have consistency with language and criteria.	F CT

Analyzing Data by Identifying Themes

Data: Teacher Responses	Theme Codes
6. I've <u>revised my rubric (after creation and use)</u>. I've learned how this can be used as <u>an instructional device</u>.	CT A
7. Though I have not adjusted practice yet, I will be looking at how I can <u>change my feedback to be tailored to the needs of specific teachers</u> and to the specific strengths and struggles of teachers' instructional practice.	F

Theme	Summary Statement
Changing thinking about assessment (A)	3 teachers' responses focused on changing thinking about assessment
Focusing on the feedback process (F)	3 teachers' responses focused on the feedback process
Using classroom assessment tools, such as rubrics, checklists, and conference notes (CT)	4 teachers' responses focused on using classroom assessment tools
Sharing with colleagues (SC)	1 teacher's response focused on sharing with colleagues

Section 6

Example 2 of Coding Data

Question: What are students' questions focused on?

Data source: 1st graders' questions for book clubs

THEME KEY

Theme	Code
Character actions	CA
Character relationships	CR
Character emotions	CE
Reader's prediction	RP
Reader's response to the book	RR

Data: Student Questions (verbatim)	Theme Codes
1. Do you think Chester Lilly and Wilson will <u>make friends</u> with Victor? Why?	CR
2. What do you think will <u>happen in the next book</u> when victor comes to town	RP
3. <u>Why do you think that the big boys were scared</u> of lillys discise	CE
4. What did <u>Chester eat</u> for breakfast?	CA
5. Why are <u>Chesterr and Wilson best friends</u>.	CR
6. What did <u>Chester Wilson and Lilly do together</u>?	CA
7. Why do you think <u>Chester, Wilson and lilly all did the same thing</u>? Explain why you think this.	CR
8. In what part doos <u>Chester and Wilison and lilly realy connct.</u>	CR
9. What do you think <u>Cheaster lilly and willson thoutht</u> when they saw victor	CE

Data: Student Questions (verbatim)	Theme Codes
10. What do you think Chester felt when lilly moved to the neighborhood?	CE
11. What do you think Victor will do?	CA
12. Do you think that Lilly is a good friend? Why?	CR
13. What do you think is going to happen with victor?	RP
14. What did Lilly teach Chester and Wilson?	CA
15. What was lily wearing and what color is it?	CA
16. What was lilly, chester, Wilson for Halloween?	CA
17. What was your favorite part in the book?	RR
18. What kind of relationship does lilly, Chester and Wilson have?	CR
19. What things did chester and Wilson do together?	CA

Source: Used with permission from Melodie Mashel, Robert J. Christen School, Bronx, N.Y.

Theme	Summary Statement
Character actions (CA)	7 questions focused on the actions of the characters
Character relationships (CR)	6 questions focused on the relationships between the characters
Character emotions (CE)	3 questions focused on the characters' emotions/ feelings
Reader's prediction (RP)	2 questions focused on the reader's prediction
Reader's response to the book (RR)	1 question focused on the reader's response to the book (favorite part)

Section 6

Drawing Conclusions from Data

The final steps in the data analysis process—describing the data, drawing conclusions, and thinking about implications—can move a group toward answering its inquiry questions, taking new action, or generating new and more significant questions.

Whenever the inquiry group is seeking to learn from the data it has collected, you can use the analysis process described in this tool. In drawing conclusions, you should be able to determine whether they are well supported or tentative. The data may reveal implications readily or lead you to ask new questions.

This tool, which you can use with both exploratory and action-oriented inquiry (see "Two Types of Inquiry: Exploratory and Action Oriented" on page 72), works best with a single data set at a time.

USING THE TOOL

1. As a group, describe specifics from the data. (These could be the summary statements you generated from "Analyzing Data by Identifying Themes" on page 158.) Statements should accurately describe or summarize, but they should not draw conclusions or hypothesize causes or next steps. For example, the group might make statements like

    -   27 out of 29 students got question #7 wrong on the test.
    -   Teachers with less than three years of experience asked the most questions on the survey.
    -   Only one student asked a question during the lesson.

2. For each of the descriptive statements, or for the ones that are most intriguing to the group, draw conclusions.

    -   If the group agrees that a conclusion is sound, then it may reveal an implication for practice and the group can list that in the third column.
    -   If a conclusion is tentative, the group may then raise another question.

Section 6

3. After reviewing the conclusions, identify as a group the implications for your study or actions, as well as any new questions you may want to pursue.

Drawing Conclusions from Data

Description of Data	Tentative Conclusions	Implications or New Questions

Examples of Drawing Conclusions from Data

Description of Data	Tentative Conclusions	Implications or New Questions
Only 1 teacher asked a metacognitive question.	• Teachers may not see metacognition as part of the curriculum. • Teachers may not have time to engage students in meta-cognitive thinking.	• Are teachers fostering meta-cognition in other ways? • How can we help teachers understand the importance of metacognition?
27 out of 29 students got question #7 wrong on the test.	• That test item was confusing. OR • The teacher did not teach the concept embedded in the question.	• Review that test item. • Examine the teacher lesson plans from the unit. • Retest students with a similar question about that concept.
Only 1 student asked a question during the lesson.	• Students didn't have any questions. • Students are used to being passive and just taking notes. • Teacher doesn't encourage questioning.	• Would we see this pattern in other lessons? What about in other classrooms?

Capturing the Group's Learning from Data Analysis

Data analysis sheds light on the practices the inquiry group is studying, and you should take time to reflect on what you have learned from the data and articulate how the learning will affect your inquiry.

This tool provides several prompts to guide reflection and allows a group to document its changing thinking. At any point you've learned from data, these prompts will serve to unpack the groups' new thinking and provide direction for next steps.

USING THE TOOL

1. Individual group members respond to each prompt privately and in writing.

2. Select one group member to keep track of new thinking that emerges from the group conversation.

3. Group members share responses to each prompt and discuss similarities and differences in their thinking and learning.

Section 6

Reflection Questions About Data Analysis

1. What themes emerged, if any, from the data we analyzed?

2. Of these themes, which seem to be most important? Why?

3. What do the data reveal that is related to our inquiry question?

4. What do the data reveal that is unrelated to the original focus but that may be important to pay attention to?

5. What new questions—about our inquiry focus or about the data itself—do I or does the group have?

6. What changes, if any, do we need to make to our research questions, actions, or data collection plan? Why might these changes be necessary?

Personal Learning Journal 6

A personal learning journal allows individual group members to reflect on their own deepening understanding of the work they are engaged in. The questions in this journal prompt provide you with an opportunity to reflect on the work the group has done with data collection and analysis.

The journal can be a private thinking tool or, if individuals share after writing, a jumping-off point for group reflection. The journal can be on paper or posted to an online discussion board so that group members can see and respond to one another's thinking.

USING THE TOOL

1. The facilitator of the group meeting (see "Facilitating Collegial Inquiry" on page 122) provides the questions to members of the group and explains that they may respond to all or some of the questions.

    • If you use the journal during a group meeting, provide enough time for thoughtful response.

2. (Optional) Allow for the sharing of individual reflection at the end of a meeting, at the start of a meeting, or between sessions via a discussion board, Google Group, or electronic mailing list.

Section 6

Personal Learning Journal 6

1. What has my group learned in the process of collecting and analyzing data?

2. How is data analysis helping us move forward?

3. What answers are emerging?

4. What new questions is my group currently pondering?

5. What have I learned about the value of data for the inquiry process?

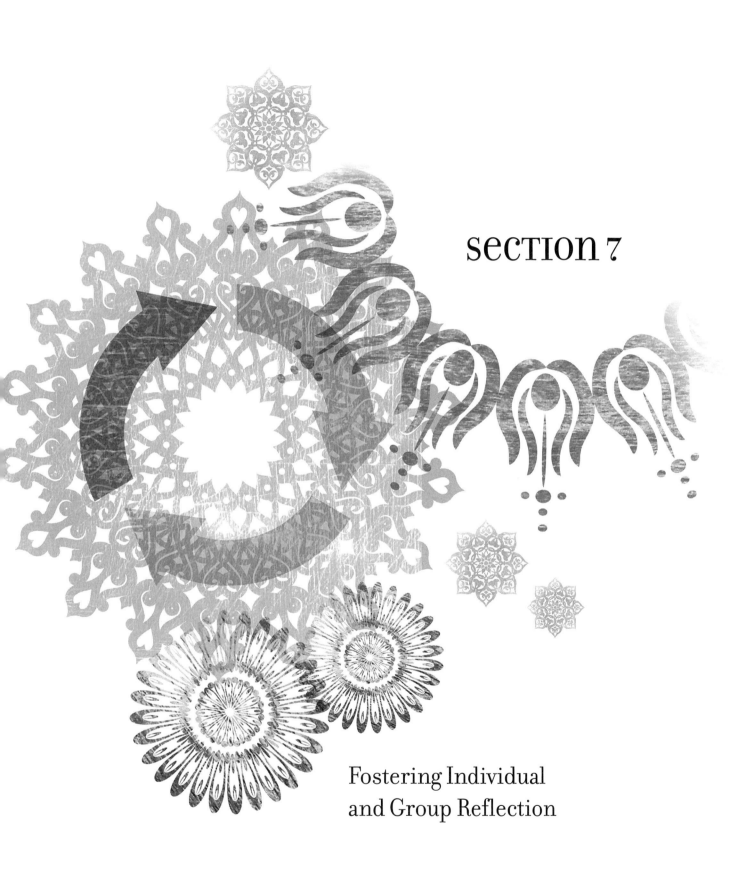

SECTION 7

Fostering Individual
and Group Reflection

SECTION 7

Fostering Individual and Group Reflection

Gauging the Group's Feelings 178

Thinking About the Inquiry Process Together 180

Reflecting Creatively 182

Ranking Actions for Value 186

Reflecting in Small Groups 188

Reflecting on Successes 190

Personal Learning Journal 7 193

177

Section 7

Gauging the Group's Feelings

Group members' feelings about their work can indicate how well their work is progressing, what is working, and what might be problematic. Sharing the underlying reasons for those feelings will allow you to process what others are experiencing.

You can use this tool to start or wrap up a meeting. Group members can also complete the handout before a meeting and bring it for discussion.

USING THE TOOL

1. Working individually, fill out the "Getting In Touch with Your Feelings" handout.
2. Post your reflection sheets for others to read. In reading others' responses, look for themes or patterns in how the group is feeling.
3. As a group, discuss any successes, issues, or problems that the reflections reveal.

Source: Used with permission from Giselle O. Martin-Kniep, Learner-Centered Initiatives Ltd., Floral Park, N.Y.

Gauging the Group's Feelings

Getting In Touch with Your Feelings

How are you feeling about the work we are doing? Circle an image or draw your own in the box. Then, complete the sentence below.

I feel this way because…

Source: Used with permission from Giselle O. Martin-Kniep, Learner-Centered Initiatives Ltd., Floral Park, N.Y.

Thinking About the Inquiry Process Together

Finding out what an inquiry group is understanding and confused about in terms of the inquiry process itself can help you determine next steps, identify needed adjustments, or identify a need for additional resources to address confusions.

By understanding the process, you can also use it in other contexts to address needs or improve practice, which builds your capacity for growth and change. You can use this tool to start or wrap up a meeting.

USING THE TOOL

1. The facilitator of the group (see "Facilitating Collegial Inquiry" on page 122) presents the first prompt and asks group members to jot down their responses.

2. After 2–3 minutes, individuals share verbally and the facilitator documents the group's responses.

3. After everyone has responded to the first question, talk as a group about what you believe needs discussion.

4. Repeat the process with the second prompt.

Thinking About the Inquiry Process Together

Group Reflection Questions About Collegial Inquiry

1. What have you learned about the nature of the collegial inquiry process from the work thus far? What are you more clear about?

2. What lingering questions do you have about the collegial inquiry process? What are you confused about or wondering about?

Section 7

Reflecting Creatively

For many, thinking nonrationally—that is, more creatively through visuals or metaphor—comes more naturally than thinking rationally and allows them to process and reflect more comfortably and thoroughly.[1]

To compliment the more straightforward, reason-based reflection that a group engages in, this tool asks you to reflect using the right, or the more intuitive, side of your brain. The tool, which you can use at the start or end of a meeting, is particularly useful when a group's work has come to an end or is wrapping up for the year.

USING THE TOOL

Before the Meeting

1. The facilitator of the meeting (see "Facilitating Collegial Inquiry" on page 122) finds 10–15 photos or images that could represent a wide range of views on the nature of collegial inquiry. Images should represent process, cycles, teamwork, reflection, or questioning work well.

At the Meeting

2. Working alone, in pairs, or in triads, review all of the reflection options and select the one you are most comfortable with.

3. For 10–15 minutes, the small groups reflect and complete the activity they chose.

4. Share or post the group's responses. As a group, highlight similarities or differences in your responses or ask questions of one another.

---

[1] Korthagen, F. A. (1993). Two modes of reflection. *Teacher and Teacher Education, 9*(3), 317–326. doi:10.1016/0742-051X(93)90046-J

Creative Reflection

Individuals, Pairs, or Triads: Pick one of the options.

OPTION 1: EXTENDED METAPHOR

Complete the sentence starter below. Elaborate on how the metaphor compares to the inquiry process with specific details and references to the work you have engaged in.

> **Engaging in collegial inquiry is like…**

OPTION 2: PHOTO OR IMAGE

Select the photo or image that you believe represents the nature of collegial inquiry. Write a brief explanation of why you selected it.

> **I chose this image because…**

Reflecting Creatively

OPTION 3: BUMPER STICKER

Identify a key insight or question related to collegial inquiry, and convey a message about it in a bumper sticker.

OPTION 4: SIX-WORD NOVEL

Identify a key insight or question related to collegial inquiry, and convey a message about it in a six-word novel.

Examples:

Struggling readers. Different strategies. Seeing success.

Different perspectives raise questions. Thinking differently.

Reflecting Creatively

OPTION 5: ROAD SIGN

Identify a key insight or question related to collegial inquiry, and convey a message about it by designing a road sign (a visual with minimal language).

Examples

Ranking Actions for Value

After a series of inquiry group meetings, you'll have carried out a number of activities, some of which you'll have completed and some of which may be ongoing. By reflecting on the actions you have taken, you can identify which types of activities promote learning and satisfaction and plan for them again. Similarly, you can identify activities that have not been as valuable, discuss why that might have been the case, and reconsider those activities.

This reflection tool guides you in reflecting on the value of specific activities you have engaged in over the course of your study together. You can also use the tool at the end of the inquiry cycle to reflect on the group's activities overall.

USING THE TOOL

1. The facilitator of the group (see "Facilitating Collegial Inquiry" on page 122) makes a list of activities the group has engaged in over time, or the group reviews past agendas and makes the list together.

2. Individually, select the three activities that had the most value for you, ranking them in order of value and explaining why you chose and ordered the activities as you did.

3. Share your rankings with the group by posting your sheet and reading others.

4. As a group, discuss your reflection using the following questions:

    • Which activities were ranked the highest by the group? Why?

    • What didn't we site as valuable? Why?

Ranking the Value of Inquiry Actions

As a group, review the specific activities you engaged in as a collegial inquiry team. (You can make a list together or refer back to past agendas.)

Individually, identify three specific activities from the list that were most valuable for you. Rank them in order of value—with 1 being "of greatest value"—and provide your reasoning for the ranking.

Ranking	Activity	Why was this of value?
1		
2		
3		

Reflecting in Small Groups

When an inquiry group is larger (more than six or seven people), it can helpful to break into smaller groups to reflect on and process learning. This allows every person to think and contribute to a discussion that follows.

This reflection tool is designed for verbal reflection, with members thinking and talking together, and it can be especially effective for group members who are more comfortable thinking through dialogue. The tool is generic enough to use at almost any point in a group's journey.

USING THE TOOL

1. Divide into small groups of no more than five members each, and take 5–10 minutes to respond to the prompts in the four quadrants.
2. So that you can easily share with the whole group, record your thinking on chart paper, modeling the four-quadrant format shown in "Small-Group Reflection."
3. Groups share their thinking, quadrant by quadrant, noting similarities and differences.
4. Based on the group's thinking, revisit your inquiry plan to see if you want to revise it or add questions, data, or actions.

Small-Group Reflection

Share what you have learned, what you have struggled with, and new questions that have emerged.

Insights Related to Our Research Questions	Insights About Our Practice
Insights About Our Students	**New or Persistent Questions**

Reflecting on Successes

Taking time to think about successes, moments when the group is working effectively, or experiences that produce important learning can help a group continue to be successful. Often we pay more attention to trouble spots than to successes, but a group can benefit greatly from dissecting just why something works, is valuable, or produces important learning.

This tool is a group, verbal reflection, and you can use it whenever the group feels it has had a success or particularly productive meeting or is energized and excited about the work it is doing.

USING THE TOOL

1. As a group, identify your success and list the specific actions, attitudes, and beliefs that supported it. The facilitator (see "Facilitating Collegial Inquiry" on page 122) should keep a list of the group's thinking.

2. Identify the environmental, social, political, or economic conditions under which the success occurred.

3. Discuss the lessons you can take away and any implications the reflection might have on future work or decisions.

Reflecting on Successes

1. What have we done right? How do we know?

2. What specific actions, attitudes, or conditions contributed to our success?

Actions	Attitudes/Beliefs	Conditions

3. What lessons can we take away from this?

Example of Reflecting on Successes

1. What have we done right? How do we know?

    We were able to analyze data together successfully. We know this because

    - We were engaged through the entire data session.
    - Some commented on the value of the work.
    - Two people said that they recognized what changes they need to make in their classrooms.
    - Our work produced several key insights and a few more good questions.
    - Time went really fast.
    - We feel as though we are making progress.

2. What specific actions, attitudes, or conditions contributed to our success?

Actions	Attitudes/Beliefs	Conditions
<ul><li>We shared the work.</li><li>We were organized at the start.</li><li>We worked in diverse groups so that we would get different perspectives.</li><li>We were flexible.</li><li>We practiced together first.</li><li>We tracked our questions as we worked.</li><li>We had enough knowledge to operate.</li><li>We were accountable to one another.</li></ul>	<ul><li>Each person in the room has expertise that is valuable.</li><li>Everyone in the building wants students to be successful; we all have that in common.</li><li>Self-directed learning is important for adult learners.</li><li>Our understanding of the context and culture of our workplace supports our success.</li><li>We have a shared understanding of our goals.</li><li>We respect one another's different working styles.</li></ul>	<ul><li>We had enough time.</li><li>We had a workspace that allowed us to spread out the data.</li><li>Our leadership supports this work.</li><li>We chose to do this work.</li></ul>

Personal Learning Journal 7

A personal learning journal allows individual group members to reflect on their own deepening understanding of the work they are engaged in. The questions in this journal prompt provide you with an opportunity to consider the work the group has done related to ongoing reflection.

The journal can be a private thinking tool or, if individuals share after writing, a jumping-off point for group reflection. The journal can be on paper or posted to an online discussion board so that group members can see and respond to one another's thinking.

USING THE TOOL

1. The facilitator of the group meeting (see "Facilitating Collegial Inquiry" on page 122) provides the questions to members of the group and explains that they may respond to all or some of the questions.

   • If you use the journal during a group meeting, provide enough time for thoughtful response.

2. (Optional) Allow for the sharing of individual reflection at the end of a meeting, at the start of a meeting, or between sessions via a discussion board, Google Group, or electronic mailing list.

Personal Learning Journal 7

1. When and how often is our group using reflection? Is it enough to capture our changing thinking?

2. Is the group varying the type of reflection it uses? Why or why not?

3. Do we need to adjust how we reflect and document our thinking? What might we do differently?

About the Author

Diane Cunningham has been an educator for 26 years, working with teachers and administrators as a professional developer for the last 16 years. Her tenure as a consultant at Learner-
Centered Initiatives Ltd. has taken her to many schools, districts, teacher centers, and Boards
of Cooperative Educational Services (BOCES) in New York State, where she has facilitated
long-term professional development programs. Her work with educators has focused on
standards-based curriculum, instruction and assessment, building capacity for professional
learning communities, supporting facilitation of adult learners, and collegial inquiry.

Cunningham has always been a strong advocate of collegial inquiry and action research,
and she has guided many educators, both preservice and in-service, through the process of
planning and carrying out collaborative and individual inquiry that is rigorous and grounded
in classroom practices. Her passion for inquiry has led her most recently to present at the
National Staff Development Council's 2010 National Conference and at the 2009 Long
Island ASCD conference.

Some of Cunningham's work related to portfolios and action research is published in *Why
Am I Doing This? Purposeful Teaching Through Portfolio Assessment* and *Becoming a Better
Teacher: Eight Innovations That Work.*

RELATED ASCD RESOURCES: ACTION RESEARCH

At the time of publication, the following ASCD resources were available (ASCD stock numbers appear in parentheses). For up-to-date information about ASCD resources, go to www.ascd.org.

ASCD EDge Group

Exchange ideas and connect with other educators interested in action research and professional learning communities on the ASCD EDge™ social networking site. Visit http://groups.ascd.org/groups/search and look for "Action Research and PLCs."

Online Courses

Schools as Professional Learning Communities: An Introduction by Vera Blake and Diane L. Jackson (#PD09OC28)

Print Products

Becoming a Better Teacher: Eight Innovations That Work by Giselle O. Martin-Kniep (#100043). Also available as PDF e-book.

Building Teachers' Capacity for Success: A Collaborative Approach for Coaches and School Leaders by Pete Hall and Alisa Simeral (#109002). Also available as PDF e-book.

Educators as Learners: Creating a Professional Learning Community in Your School by Michael S. Castleberry and Penelope J. Wald (#100005). Also available as PDF e-book.

Guiding School Improvement with Action Research by Richard Sagor (#100047). Also available as PDF e-book.

How to Conduct Collaborative Action Research by Richard Sagor (#61193011). Also available as PDF e-book.

How to Use Action Research in the Self-Renewing School by Emily F. Calhoun (#194030E4). E-book only.

Teacher-Centered Professional Development by Gabriel Diaz-Maggioli (#104021). Also available as PDF e-book.

Protocols for Professional Learning (The Professional Learning Community Series) by Lois Brown Easton (#109037). Also available as PDF e-book.

Strengthening and Enriching Your Professional Learning Community: The Art of Learning Together by Geoffrey Caine and Renate N. Caine (#110085)

Professional Interest Communities

Visit the ASCD website (www.ascd.org) and click on "Prof. Interest Communities" under the "Community" tab in the left-hand navigation for information about professional educators who have formed groups around topics like "Interdisciplinary Curriculum and Instruction" and "Mentoring Leadership and Resource." Look in the Professional Interest Communities Directory for current facilitators' e-mail addresses.

For more information: send e-mail to member@ascd.org; call 1-800-933-2723 or 1-703-578-9600, press 1; send a fax to 1-703-575-5400; or write to Information Services, ASCD, 1703 N. Beauregard St., Alexandria, VA 22311-1714 USA.